# The Low Cholesterol
## 150 Delicious R
## to Help Reduce Bad Fats
## and Lower Your Cholesterol
## Without Prescription Drugs

by **Vesela Tabakova**
Text copyright(c)2021 Vesela Tabakova

All rights reserved. No part of this publication may be reproduced, distributed, or transmitted in any form or by any means, including photocopying, recording, or other electronic or mechanical methods, without the prior written permission of the publisher, except in the case of brief quotations embodied in critical reviews and certain other noncommercial uses permitted by copyright law.

Although every precaution has been taken to verify the accuracy of the information contained herein, the author and publisher assume no responsibility for any errors or omissions. No liability is assumed for damages that may result from the use of information contained within.

## Table Of Contents

| | |
|---|---|
| Healthy Eating Tips to Lower Cholesterol | 7 |
| Lifestyle changes to help lower cholesterol | 8 |
| Heart Healthy Salads and Appetizers | 9 |
| Greek Barley Salad | 10 |
| Spring Salad | 11 |
| Tuna Salad | 12 |
| Red Cabbage Salad | 13 |
| Roasted Peppers with Garlic and Parsley | 14 |
| Chicken and Iceberg Lettuce Salad | 15 |
| Creamy Chicken and Pasta Salad | 16 |
| Spinach and Barley Salad | 17 |
| Roasted Leek and Sweet Potato Salad | 18 |
| Mediterranean Avocado Salad | 19 |
| Avocado and Cucumber Salad | 20 |
| Warm Vitamin Salad | 21 |
| Apple, Walnut and Radicchio Salad | 22 |
| Beetroot and Carrot Salad with Salmon and Egg | 23 |
| Apple, Celery and Walnut Salad | 24 |
| Fresh Greens Salad | 25 |
| Beet Salad with Spinach and Walnuts | 26 |
| Beet and Lentil Salad | 27 |
| Bulgarian Chicken Salad | 28 |
| Green Pea and Chicken Salad | 29 |
| Beet and Bean Sprout Salad | 30 |
| Roasted Vegetable Salad | 31 |
| Light Superfood Salad | 32 |
| Quinoa Chicken Salad | 33 |
| Baby Spinach Salad | 34 |
| Roasted Pumpkin and Spinach Salad | 35 |
| Green Bean and Radicchio Salad with Green Olive Dressing | 37 |
| Easy Green Bean Salad | 38 |
| Three Bean Salad | 39 |
| Balsamic Chicken and White Bean Salad | 40 |
| Salmon Macaroni Salad Recipe | 41 |
| White Bean and Tuna Salad | 42 |

| | |
|---|---:|
| Warm Quinoa Salad | 43 |
| Quinoa and Black Bean Salad | 44 |
| Roasted Vegetable Quinoa Salad | 45 |
| Quinoa with Oven Roasted Tomatoes and Pesto | 46 |
| Cucumber Quinoa Salad | 48 |
| Fresh Vegetable Quinoa Salad | 49 |
| Warm Mushroom Quinoa Salad | 50 |
| Artichoke and Mushroom Salad | 51 |
| Quinoa and Asparagus Salad | 52 |
| Warm Cauliflower and Quinoa Salad | 53 |
| Quinoa, Zucchini and Carrot Salad | 54 |
| Tabbouleh | 55 |
| Fatoush | 56 |
| Greek Salad with Avocado | 57 |
| The Best Orzo Salad | 58 |
| Heart Healthy Soups | 59 |
| Mediterranean Chicken Soup | 60 |
| Greek Lemon Chicken Soup | 61 |
| Fresh Asparagus Soup | 62 |
| Creamy Red Lentil Soup | 63 |
| Lentil, Barley and Kale Soup | 64 |
| Spinach and Mushrooms Soup | 65 |
| Broccoli and Potato Soup | 66 |
| Moroccan Lentil Soup | 67 |
| Hearty Italian Minestrone | 68 |
| Moroccan Chicken and Butternut Squash Soup | 69 |
| Chicken Soup with Vermicelli | 71 |
| French Vegetable Soup | 72 |
| Beetroot and Carrot Soup | 73 |
| Celery, Apple and Carrot Soup | 74 |
| Monastery Style White Bean Soup | 75 |
| Fish and Noodle Soup | 76 |
| Hearty Lamb and Vegetable Soup | 77 |
| Creamy Cauliflower Soup | 78 |
| Pumpkin and Bell Pepper Soup | 79 |
| Creamy Potato Soup | 80 |

| | |
|---|---|
| Shredded Cabbage Soup | 81 |
| Easy Fish Soup | 82 |
| Spanish Seafood Soup | 84 |
| Hot Spanish Squid Soup | 86 |
| Mediterranean Chickpea Soup | 87 |
| Wild Mushroom Soup | 88 |
| Thick Herb Soup | 89 |
| Spanish Gazpacho Soup | 90 |
| Avocado Gazpacho | 91 |
| Cold Cucumber Soup | 92 |
| Spinach Soup | 93 |
| Brussels Sprouts and Potato Soup | 94 |
| Brussels Sprouts and Tomato Soup | 95 |
| Tomato and Quinoa Soup | 96 |
| Spinach, Leek and Quinoa Soup | 97 |
| Vegetable Quinoa Soup | 98 |
| Heart Healthy Main Dish Recipes | 99 |
| Mediterranean Chicken Casserole | 100 |
| Chicken and Potato Casserole | 101 |
| Easy Chicken Parmigiana | 102 |
| Mediterranean Chicken Drumstick Casserole | 103 |
| Mediterranean Lamb Casserole | 104 |
| Lamb and Potato Casserole | 106 |
| Avocado and Rocket Pasta | 107 |
| Delicious Broccoli Pasta | 108 |
| Creamy Butternut Squash Spaghetti | 109 |
| Sweet Potato Spaghetti | 110 |
| Quick Orzo and Zucchini Dinner | 112 |
| Best Vegan Pizza | 113 |
| Cheesy Potato and Zucchini Bake | 114 |
| Crispy Feta Cheese Pastry | 115 |
| Pesto Chicken | 116 |
| Greek Chicken And Lemon Rice | 117 |
| Spicy Chicken and Bean Stew | 119 |
| Mushroom and Spinach Scrambled Eggs | 120 |
| Feta and Olive Scrambled Eggs | 121 |

| | |
|---|---|
| Spinach Omelet | 122 |
| Greek Chicken Casserole | 123 |
| Hunter Style Chicken | 124 |
| Sweet and Sour Sicilian Chicken | 125 |
| Moroccan Chicken Casserole | 126 |
| Chicken Moussaka | 128 |
| Eggplant and Chickpea Stew | 130 |
| Green Pea and Mushroom Stew | 131 |
| Tomato Leek Stew | 132 |
| Potato and Leek Stew | 133 |
| Spinach with Rice | 134 |
| Rich Vegetable Stew | 135 |
| Hearty Baked Beans | 136 |
| Rice Stuffed Bell Peppers | 137 |
| Bell Peppers Stuffed with Beans | 138 |
| Stuffed Grapevine Leaves | 139 |
| Stuffed Cabbage Leaves | 141 |
| Green Bean and Potato Stew | 143 |
| Cabbage and Rice Stew | 144 |
| Rice with Leeks and Olives | 145 |
| Rice and Tomato Stew | 146 |
| Roasted Cauliflower | 147 |
| New Potatoes with Herbs | 148 |
| Potato and Zucchini Bake | 149 |
| Baked Mediterranean Casserole with Tofu and Feta Cheese | 150 |
| Okra and Tomato Casserole | 151 |
| Roasted Cauliflower | 152 |
| Roasted Brussels Sprouts | 153 |
| Roasted Butternut Squash | 154 |
| Roasted Artichoke Hearts | 155 |
| Beet Fries | 156 |
| Grilled Vegetable Skewers | 157 |
| Heart Healthy Breakfasts and Desserts | 158 |
| Raisin Quinoa Breakfast | 159 |
| Citrus Quinoa Breakfast | 160 |
| Avocado and Olive Paste on Toasted Rye Bread | 161 |

| | |
|---|---:|
| Avocado, Lettuce and Tomato Sandwiches | 162 |
| Avocado and Chickpea Sandwiches | 163 |
| Winter Greens Smoothie | 164 |
| Delicious Kale Smoothie | 165 |
| Cherry Smoothie | 166 |
| Banana and Coconut Smoothie | 167 |
| Vegan Walnut Pie | 168 |
| Baked Apples | 169 |
| Blueberry Yogurt Dessert | 170 |
| Fresh Strawberries in Mascarpone and Rose Water | 171 |
| Apple Cake | 172 |
| Pumpkin Baked with Dry Fruit | 173 |
| Pumpkin Pastry | 174 |
| Apple Pastry | 175 |
| Pumpkin Cake | 176 |
| Granny's Vegan Cake | 177 |
| About the Author | 178 |

# Healthy Eating Tips to Lower Cholesterol

Cholesterol is a waxy fat-like substance produced naturally in the liver and used by our body to make hormones, vitamin D, and substances that help us digest foods. Cholesterol can also be absorbed by the intestines when eating foods deriving from animal sources such as egg yolks, meat, and cheese.
Cholesterol is not inherently "bad" but too much of it can pose a problem because it sometimes forms fatty deposits in our arteries which could affect the heart. While high cholesterol can be inherited, it's often the result of unhealthy lifestyle choices, which makes it treatable and preventable.

Cholesterol comes in two forms - Low-density lipoprotein (LDL), which we call bad cholesterol, and High-density lipoprotein (HDL), or good cholesterol.

LDL is considered bad because it builds up inside artery walls and raises our chances of heart disease. HDL, on the other hand, takes the "bad" cholesterol into the liver where it is processed and eliminated. Together with tryglicerides, which are another form of blood fat, LDL and HDL form our total cholesterol count. When HDL is high and LDL is low, our body is healthier.

Being overweight, lack of exercise, an unhealthy diet high in processed foods, animal fats and sugar, plus smoking and drinking alcohol can all play a role in raising our cholesterol. Usually, high cholesterol does not produce any symptoms but if it is is too high, it can increase the risk for serious conditions such as high blood pressure, heart attack and stroke.

The good news is that there is a way we can improve our cholesterol levels without resorting to medication. If we follow just a few easy guidelines, we can control and balance our bad cholesterol and these simple lifestyle changes can further contribute to lowering our risk of other illnesses or prevent existing conditions from getting worse.

# Lifestyle changes to help lower cholesterol

**Eat less meat.** Select lean cuts of meat with minimal visible fat or trim all visible fat from meat before cooking. Limit processed meats such as sausage, bologna, salami and hot dogs. Processed meats, even those with "reduced fat" labels, are high in saturated fat.

**Eat more fish.** Even fatty fish is low in saturated fat.

**Eat more foods known to lower cholesterol.** Cook them in a tiny bit of olive oil and add herbs and spices to make meals even tastier. Foods known to lower cholesterol are affordable and easy to to find. Legumes, oats, barley, okra, and eggplant, soy protein, olives, avocados and tree nuts such as almonds, walnuts, pecans, hazelnuts and cashews are all rich in soluble fiber and good fats and an excellent choice when trying to lower cholesterol naturally. Herbs and spices are nutritional powerhouses packed with vitamins, minerals and antioxidants. Studies have shown that garlic, turmeric and ginger are especially effective at lowering cholesterol when eaten regularly.

**Eat more fruits and vegetables.** They have no cholesterol at all, they have good, healthy fats and contain high levels of antioxidants and phyto-sterols which bind with bad cholesterol within the intestines and reduce its absorption.

**Limit alcohol.** Too much alcohol harms the liver and adds extra calories, which can lead to weight gain. Being overweight can raise your LDL levels and lowers your HDL levels.

**Exercise and lose weight.** Any type of exercise improves cholesterol and promotes heart health. The longer the exercise, the greater the benefit.

**Decrease stress levels.** When our bodies are under long term stress we have high levels of stress hormones which cause high blood cholesterol.

# Heart Healthy Salads and Appetizers

# Greek Barley Salad

*Serves: 4*
*Ingredients:*

2/3 cup quick-cooking barley

2-3 green onions, thinly sliced

1 small cucumber, diced

2 green peppers, diced

2 tomatoes, diced

2 tbsp chopped fresh parsley

1 tsp capers, drained and rinsed

juice of ½ a lemon

2 tsp olive oil

1 tsp balsamic vinegar

salt and pepper, to taste

a pinch of dried oregano

*Directions:*

Cook barley according to package directions.

In a medium bowl, toss together the barley, green onions, cucumber, green peppers, tomatoes, parsley, capers and lemon juice.

In a smaller bowl, stir together the remaining ingredients and pour over the salad. Toss to combine and serve.

# Spring Salad

*Serves: 4*
*Ingredients:*

1 green lettuce, washed and drained

1 cucumber, sliced

a bunch of radishes, sliced

a bunch of spring onions, finely cut

juice of half lemon or 2 tbsp of white wine vinegar

3 tbsp olive oil

salt, to taste

*Directions:*

Cut the lettuce into thin strips. Slice the cucumber and the radishes as thinly as possible and chop the spring onions.

Combine all salad ingredients in a large bowl, add the lemon juice and olive oil and season with salt to taste.

# Tuna Salad

*Serves 4*
*Ingredients:*

1 head green lettuce, washed and drained

1 cucumber, cut

1 tuna can, drained and cut into medium chunks

½ cup canned sweet corn, drained

5-6 radishes

2-3 spring onions

3-4 tbsp lemon juice

2 tbsp olive oil

salt, to taste

Cut the lettuce into thin strips. Slice the cucumber and the radishes as thinly as possible and chop the spring onions.

Mix all the vegetables in a large bowl, add the tuna and the sweet corn and season with lemon juice, olive oil and salt to taste.

# Red Cabbage Salad

*Serves: 6*
*Ingredients:*

1 small head red cabbage, cored and chopped

1 bunch of fresh dill, finely cut

3 tbsp olive oil

3 tbsp red wine vinegar

2 tsp salt

black pepper, to taste

*Directions:*

In a small bowl, mix the oil, red wine vinegar, and black pepper.

Place the cabbage in a larger glass bowl. Sprinkle the salt on top and crunch it with your hands to soften.

Pour the dressing over the cabbage and toss to coat.

Sprinkle with dill, cover with foil and leave in the refrigerator for half an hour before serving.

# Roasted Peppers with Garlic and Parsley

*Serves: 4-6*
*Ingredients:*

2.25 lb red and green bell peppers

3-4 garlic cloves, chopped

4 tbsp olive oil

2 tbsp white wine vinegar

1 cup finely cut fresh parsley

salt and pepper, to taste

*Directions:*

Grill the peppers or roast them in the oven at 480 F until the skins are a little burnt. Peel the skins and remove the seeds. Cut the peppers into strips lengthwise and layer them in a bowl.

Mix together the oil, vinegar, salt and pepper, chopped garlic and chopped parsley leaves. Pour over the peppers. Cover the roasted peppers and chill for an hour.

# Chicken and Iceberg Lettuce Salad

*Serves 4*
*Ingredients:*

1 cup cooked chicken breasts, coarsely chopped

1/2 head iceberg lettuce, halved and chopped

1 avocado, peeled, pitted and chopped

1 celery rib, chopped

1 small apple, peeled and chopped

1/2 red bell pepper, deseeded and chopped

9-10 green olives, pitted and halved

1/2 red onion, sliced

**for the dressing:**

2 tbsp olive oil

1 tbsp honey

2 tbsp lemon juice

salt and pepper, to taste

*Directions:*

Cut all the vegetables and toss them, together with the olives, in a large bowl. Add in the chicken.

Prepare the salad dressing in a separate smaller bowl by mixing together the olive oil, honey and lemon juice.

Season with salt and pepper, to taste, and serve.

# Creamy Chicken and Pasta Salad

*Serves 4*
*Prep time: 5 min*

*Ingredients:*

2 cups small pasta, cooked

1 chicken breast, cooked and diced

1 cup cherry tomatoes, halved

1/2 cup green olives, pitted and halved

1 red pepper, chopped

1/2 red onion, sliced

3 tbsp low-fat crème fraîche

salt, to taste

*Directions:*

Place pasta, chicken, tomatoes, olives, red onion and red pepper in a salad bowl.

Add in crème fraîche and combine with the pasta, vegetables and chicken.

# Spinach and Barley Salad

*Serves: 4*
*Ingredients:*

2/3 cup quick-cooking barley

3 cups finely cut spinach leaves

7-8 cherry tomatoes, halved

2-3 green onions, cut

3 tbsp grated Parmesan cheese

*for the dressing:*

3 tbsp olive oil

2 tbsp white wine vinegar

1 garlic clove, crushed

salt and black pepper, to taste

*Directions:*

Cook barley according to package instructions

Whisk the dressing ingredients in a small bowl until smooth. Season with salt and pepper to taste.

Combine barley, spinach, tomatoes and onions in a salad bowl. Drizzle with the dressing, toss to combine, sprinkle with Parmesan cheese and serve.

# Roasted Leek and Sweet Potato Salad

*Serves: 5*
*Ingredients:*

1 lb sweet potato, unpeeled, cut into 1 inch pieces

3-4 leeks, trimmed and cut into 1 inch slices

a handful of baby spinach leaves

1 cup watercress, rinsed, patted dry and separated from roots

1 tbsp dried mint

2 tbsp olive oil

2 tbsp lemon juice

*Directions:*

Preheat oven to 350 F. Line a baking tray with baking paper and place the sweet potato and leeks on it. Drizzle with olive oil and sprinkle with mint. Toss to coat. Roast for 20 minutes or until tender.

Place roasted vegetables, baby spinach and watercress in a salad bowl and stir. Sprinkle with lemon juice and serve.

# Mediterranean Avocado Salad

*Serves: 5*
*Ingredients:*

1 avocado, peeled, halved and cut into cubes

1 cup grape tomatoes

1 cup radishes, sliced

2 tbsp drained capers, rinsed

1 large cucumber, quartered and sliced

a handful of rocket leaves

½ cup green olives, pitted, halved

½ cup black olives, pitted, sliced

7-8 fresh basil leaves, torn

2 tbsp olive oil

2 tbsp red wine vinegar

salt and pepper, to taste

*Directions:*

Place avocado, cucumber, tomatoes, radishes, rocket, olives, capers and basil in a large salad bowl.

Toss to combine then sprinkle with vinegar and olive oil. Season with salt and pepper, toss again and serve.

# Avocado and Cucumber Salad

*Serves: 5*
*Ingredients:*

2 avocados, peeled, halved and sliced

2-3 green onions, finely cut

1 cucumber, halved, sliced

1 orange, peeled and cut into cubes

1/2 cup cooked sweet corn

*for the dressing:*

2 tbsp olive oil

1 tbsp lemon juice

1 tbsp Dijon mustard

1/2 cup finely cut dill leaves

salt and pepper, to taste

*Directions:*

Combine the avocado, cucumber, orange, sweet corn and green onions in a deep salad bowl.

Whisk olive oil, lemon juice, dill and mustard until smooth, then drizzle over the salad.

Season with salt and pepper to taste, toss to combine and serve.

# Warm Vitamin Salad

*Serves: 4*
*Ingredients:*

7 oz cauliflower, cut into florets

7 oz baby Brussels sprouts, trimmed

7 oz broccoli, cut into florets

1/2 cup chopped leeks

*for the dressing:*

2 tbsp lemon juice

4 tbsp olive oil

1/2 tsp ginger powder

1/2 cup parsley leaves, very finely cut

**Directions:**

Cook cauliflower, broccoli and Brussels sprouts in a steamer basket over boiling water for 10 minutes or until just tender. Refresh under cold water for a minute and set aside in a deep salad bowl.

Whisk lemon juice, olive oil and ginger powder in a small bowl. Add in salt and pepper to taste; pour over the salad. Top with parsley and serve.

# Apple, Walnut and Radicchio Salad

*Serves: 4-5*
*Ingredients:*

1 radicchio, trimmed, finely shredded

2 apples, quartered and thinly sliced

a handful of rocket leaves

4-5 green onions, chopped

1/2 cup walnuts, halved and toasted

1 tbsp Dijon mustard

1 tbsp balsamic vinegar

3-4 tbsp olive oil

salt, to taste

*Directions:*

Prepare the dressing by combining mustard, lemon juice and olive oil.

Place walnuts on a baking tray and bake in a preheated to 400 F oven for 3-4 minutes, or until browned.

Mix radicchio, rocket, apples, onions and walnuts in a large salad bowl. Add the dressing; season with salt, toss to combine and serve.

# Beetroot and Carrot Salad with Salmon and Egg

*Serves 4*
*Ingredients:*

3 eggs, boiled and quartered

2 beets, peeled and coarsely grated

2 carrots, peeled and coarsely grated

5 oz smoked salmon, flaked

3-4 green onions, chopped

1/4 cup fresh lemon juice

2 tbsp olive oil

salt and black pepper, to taste

*Directions:*

Boil eggs over high heat for 5 minutes. Drain, cool and peel. Shred carrots and beets and divide them among serving plates. Cut each egg in quarters and place on top of the vegetables. Top with the salmon flakes.

Prepare the dressing by whisking lemon juice and oil in a small bowl. Season with salt and pepper and drizzle the dressing over the salad. Serve sprinkled with green onions.

# Apple, Celery and Walnut Salad

*Serves: 4*
*Ingredients:*

3 large apples, quartered, cores removed, thinly sliced

1 celery rib, thinly sliced

½ cup walnuts, chopped

1 red onion, thinly sliced

2 tbsp raisins

1/4 cup sunflower seeds

3 tbsp apple cider vinegar

2 tbsp olive oil

salt and black pepper, to taste

*Directions:*

Mix vinegar, olive oil, salt and pepper in a small bowl. Whisk until well combined.

Place apples, celery, onion, walnuts, raisins and sunflower seeds in a bigger salad bowl. Drizzle with dressing, toss and serve.

# Fresh Greens Salad

*Serves: 6-7*
*Ingredients:*

1 head red leaf lettuce, rinsed, dried and chopped

1 head green leaf lettuce, rinsed, dried and chopped

1 head endive, rinsed, dried and chopped

1 cup frisee lettuce leaves, rinsed, dried and chopped

3-4 fresh basil leaves, chopped

3-4 fresh mint leaves, chopped

2-3 green onions, chopped

1 tbsp chia seeds

4 tbsp olive oil

3-4 tbsp lemon juice

1 tsp sugar

salt, to taste

*Directions:*

Place the red and green leaf lettuce, frisee lettuce, endive, onions, basil and mint into a large salad bowl and toss lightly to combine.

Prepare the dressing by whisking lemon juice, olive oil and sugar and pour it over the salad. Sprinkle with chia seeds and season with salt to taste.

# Beet Salad with Spinach and Walnuts

*Serves: 4*
*Ingredients:*

3 medium beets, steamed and diced

1/2 bag baby spinach leaves

1 red onion, sliced

1/2 cup walnuts, halved and toasted

*for the dressing:*

1 garlic clove, crushed

2 tbsp lemon juice

3 tbsp olive oil

4-5 fresh mint leaves, chopped

½ tsp salt

*Directions:*

Place the beats in a steam basket set over a pot of boiling water. Steam for about 12-15 minutes, or until tender. Leave to cool for 5-6 minutes, then peel and dice the beets. Place the spinach leaves in a large salad bowl. Add in the beets, onion and walnuts.

In a smaller bowl, combine the oil, lemon juice, garlic and mint. Whisk and drizzle over the salad.

# Beet and Lentil Salad

*Serves: 6*
*Ingredients:*

1 can brown lentils, drained and rinsed

1 can pickled beets, drained and cut in cubes

5 oz baby rocket leaves

¼ cup walnuts, toasted and roughly chopped

4-5 green onions, chopped

1 garlic clove, crushed

3 tbsp olive oil

2 tbsp lemon juice

salt and black pepper, to taste

*Directions:*

Heat olive oil in a frying pan and gently sauté green onions for 1-2 minutes or until softened. Add in garlic and lentils. Cook, for 2 minutes then add in beets and cook for 2-3 minutes more.

Combine baby rocket, walnuts and lentil mixture in a large salad bowl. Sprinkle with lemon juice, toss gently to combine and serve.

# Bulgarian Chicken Salad

*Serves 6*
*Ingredients:*

2 cups cooked chicken, chopped

2 hard boiled eggs, diced

2-3 pickled gherkins, chopped

1 large apple, diced

½ cup walnuts, baked

½ cup low fat mayonnaise

1 tbsp lemon juice

salt and pepper to taste

Bake walnuts in a single layer in a preheated to 480 F oven for 5 minutes, or until toasted and fragrant, stirring halfway through.

In a bowl, stir together chicken, apple, eggs and gherkins. Combine mayonnaise, lemon juice, salt and pepper to taste and add to the chicken mixture.

Sprinkle with walnuts and serve.

# Green Pea and Chicken Salad

*Serves 4*
*Ingredients:*

2 cups chopped, cooked, chicken breast

1 cup green peas, cooked

1 medium apple, diced

2-3 green onions, finely cut

a bunch of fresh dill, finely cut

salt and ground black pepper to taste

2 tbsp lemon juice

1 tbsp olive oil

Combine all salad ingredients in a bowl and mix well. Serve chilled.

# Beet and Bean Sprout Salad

*Serves: 4-5*
*Ingredients:*

5-6 beet greens, cut in thin strips

2 tomatoes, sliced

1 cup bean sprouts, washed

3 tbsp pumpkin seeds

1 tbsp grated lemon rind

2 garlic cloves, crushed

4 tbsp lemon juice

3 tbsp olive oil

1 tsp salt

*Directions:*

In a large bowl, toss together beet greens, bean sprouts, tomatoes and pumpkin seeds.

Mix oil and lemon juice with lemon rind, salt and garlic and pour over the salad. Serve chilled.

# Roasted Vegetable Salad

*Serves: 4*
*Ingredients:*

2 tomatoes, halved

1 medium zucchini, quartered

1 eggplant, ends trimmed, quartered

2 large red pepper, halved, deseeded, cut into strips

2-3 white mushrooms, halved

1 onion, quartered

1 tsp garlic powder

2 tbsp olive oil

*for the dressing:*

1 tbsp lemon juice

1 tbsp apple cider vinegar

2 tbsp olive oil

1 tsp sumac

5 tbsp crushed walnuts, to serve

*Directions:*

Whisk olive oil, lemon juice, vinegar and sumac in a bowl.

Preheat oven to 500 F. Place the zucchini, eggplant, peppers, onion, mushrooms and tomatoes on a lined baking sheet.

Sprinkle with olive oil, season with salt, pepper and sumac and roast until golden, about 25 minutes. Divide in 4-5 plates, top with crushed walnuts, drizzle with the dressing and serve.

# Light Superfood Salad

*Serves: 4*
*Ingredients:*

1 cup mixed green salad leaves

2 cups watercress, rinsed, patted dry and separated from roots

4-5 green onions, chopped

1 avocado, peeled and cubed

10 radishes, sliced

10 green olives, pitted and halved

*for the dressing:*

1 tbsp lemon juice

2 tbsp apple cider vinegar

2 tbsp olive oil

1 tbsp Dijon mustard

1/2 tsp dried mint

*Directions:*

Combine all salad ingredients in a large bowl.

In a medium bowl or cup, whisk lemon juice, vinegar, olive oil, mint and mustard until smooth. Pour over salad, toss, and serve.

# Quinoa Chicken Salad

*Serves 6*
*Ingredients:*

1 cup quinoa

2 cups chicken breasts, cooked and chopped

½ cup black olives, pitted

1 tbsp capers, chopped

1 garlic clove, minced

2 tbsp olive oil

2 tbsp lemon juice

salt to taste

ground pepper, to taste

half a bunch fresh parsley, finely cut

Wash very well quinoa in lots of water and cook it according to package directions.

Combine olives and next 7 ingredients in a large bowl, stirring well.

Add quinoa to the bowl, mixing gently with the vegetables. Stir in chicken before serving.

# Baby Spinach Salad

*Serves: 4*
*Ingredients:*

1 bag baby spinach, washed and dried

1 red bell pepper, cut in slices

1 cup cherry tomatoes, cut in halves

1 small red onion, finely chopped

1 cup black olives, pitted

*for the dressing:*

1 tsp dried oregano

1 large garlic clove

3 tbsp red wine vinegar

4 tbsp olive oil

salt and black pepper, to taste

*Directions:*

Prepare the dressing by blending the garlic and oregano with olive oil and vinegar in a food processor.

Place the spinach leaves in a large salad bowl and toss with the dressing. Add the rest of the ingredients and give everything a toss again. Season to taste with black pepper and salt.

# Roasted Pumpkin and Spinach Salad

*Serves: 4*
*Ingredients:*

1 cup pumpkin, deseeded, peeled and cut into wedges

1/2 bag baby spinach leaves

1/2 cup canned chickpeas, drained

1/3 cup toasted hazelnuts, coarsely chopped

1 small red onion, thinly sliced

2 tbsp olive oil

2 tbsp maple syrup

*for the dressing:*

2 tbsp olive oil

2 tbsp lemon juice

1 garlic clove, crushed

salt and pepper, to taste

*Directions:*

Preheat oven to 350 F. Line a baking tray with baking paper. Place pumpkin, maple syrup and olive oil in a bowl. Toss to combine. Season with salt and pepper and toss again.

Place pumpkin, in a single layer, on prepared tray. Bake, turning once, for 20-30 minutes or until the pumpkin is tender. Set aside for to cool.

In a small bowl, whisk the dressing ingredients until smooth. Season with salt and pepper to taste.

Place the pumpkin, spinach, chickpeas, onion and hazelnuts in a large salad bowl. Drizzle with the dressing, toss, and serve.

# Green Bean and Radicchio Salad with Green Olive Dressing

*Serves: 4*
*Ingredients:*

1 lb trimmed green beans, cut to 2-3 inch long pieces

1 radicchio, outer leaves removed, washed, dried

1 small red onion, finely cut

1 cup cherry tomatoes, halved

*green olive dressing*

1/2 cup green olives, pitted

1/3 cup olive oil

2 garlic cloves, chopped

black pepper and salt, to taste

*Directions:*

Roughly tear the radicchio leaves and place on a large serving platter.

Steam or boil green beans for about 3-4 minutes until crisp-tender. In a colander, wash with cold water to stop cooking, then pat dry and arrange over the radicchio leaves. Add in red onion and cherry tomatoes.

To make the green olive dressing, place the olives in a food processor and blend until finely chopped. Gradually add the oil and process until a smooth paste is formed. Taste and season with salt and pepper then spoon over salad and serve.

# Easy Green Bean Salad

*Serves: 6*
*Ingredients:*

2 cups canned green beans, drained

1 small onion, sliced

4 garlic cloves, crushed

3-4 fresh mint leaves, chopped

a bunch of fresh dill, finely chopped

3 tbsp olive oil

1 tbsp apple cider vinegar

salt and pepper, to taste

*Directions:*

Put the green beans in a medium bowl and mix with onion, mint and dill.

In a smaller bowl, stir olive oil, vinegar, garlic, salt and pepper until smooth. Pour over the green bean mixture and serve.

# Three Bean Salad

*Serves: 4*
*Ingredients:*

½ cup canned white beans, drained and rinsed

1 lb trimmed green beans, cut to 2 inch long pieces

½ cup canned chickpeas, drained and rinsed

1 red pepper, thinly sliced

1 yellow pepper, thinly sliced

1/2 red onion, thinly sliced

*for the dressing:*

1 tbsp died basil leaves

2 tbsp olive oil

1 tsp garlic powder

1 tbsp red wine vinegar

salt, to taste

*Directions:*

Steam green beans for about 3-4 minutes until crisp-tender. Rinse with cold water, pat dry and place in a salad bowl. Mix in the chickpeas, white beans, onions and peppers.

In a small bowl, whisk together vinegar, olive oil, basil and salt. Pour over the salad, toss gently to combine and serve.

# Balsamic Chicken and White Bean Salad

*Serves 4-6*
*Ingredients:*

1 lb skinless chicken breasts

1 cup canned white beans, drained

1 cup cherry tomatoes, halved

1 cup feta cheese, crumbled

1 cup rocket leaves

2 garlic cloves, crushed

1 tbsp honey

2 tbsp balsamic vinegar

3 tbsp olive oil

*Directions:*

Whisk garlic, honey and vinegar in a deep bowl. Add chicken breasts and turn to coat. Season with salt and black pepper to taste. Cover and marinate for thirty minutes.

Preheat a barbecue plate or grill on high heat. Lightly brush chicken with oil and cook for two minutes each side or until golden. Reduce heat to medium-low and cook chicken for five minutes each side or until cooked through. Set aside in a plate, covered, for five minutes then slice.

Combine beans, tomatoes, feta cheese, rocket leaves and chicken in a salad bowl. Toss gently and serve.

# Salmon Macaroni Salad Recipe

*Serves 6*
*Ingredients:*

2 cups macaroni pasta

1 cup canned salmon, cut into medium chunks

1 red pepper, cut into strips

1/2 cup canned sweet corn, drained

1/2 cup mayonnaise

1 tsp mustard

1 tsp lemon juice

1 bunch spring onions, chopped

3 tbsp fresh parsley leaves, finely cut

1 tbsp fresh dill, finely cut

freshly ground black pepper, to taste

*Directions:*

Cook macaroni according to package directions. Remove from heat, drain, rinse briefly in cold water and drain again.

In a large bowl, mix the salmon, corn, red pepper, mayonnaise, mustard, and lemon juice. Mix in the spring onions, parsley and dill. Add the cooked macaroni while still warm. Season with freshly ground pepper to taste. Serve chilled.

# White Bean and Tuna Salad

*Serves 4*
*Ingredients:*

2 cups canned white beans, rinsed and drained

1 cup canned tuna, cut into large chunks

1 red onion, chopped

1/2 cup black olives, pitted, halved

juice of one lemon

1/2 cup fresh parsley leaves, chopped

1 tbsp dried mint

salt and freshly ground black pepper , to taste

3 tbsp olive oil

*Directions:*

Put tuna into a large bowl. Add the white beans and gently stir to combine. Add olives, onions, parsley, mint, lemon juice and olive oil and mix to combine. If the salad seems a little dry, add some more oil.

Season with salt and black pepper to taste. Serve chilled.

# Warm Quinoa Salad

*Serves: 6*
*Ingredients:*

1 cup quinoa

½ cup green beans, frozen

½ cup sweet corn, frozen

½ cup carrots, diced

½ cup black olives, pitted and halved

2-3 garlic cloves, crushed

2 tbsp fresh dill, finely cut

3 tbsp lemon juice

2 tbsp olive oil

*Directions:*

Wash quinoa with lots of water. Strain it and cook it according to package directions. When ready, set aside in a large salad bowl and fluff with a fork. Heat olive oil in a large saucepan over medium heat.

Stew green beans, sweet corn, olives and carrots until vegetables are tender. Add this mixture to quinoa and stir to combine.

In a smaller bowl, combine lemon juice, dill and garlic and pour over the warm salad. Add salt and black pepper to taste and serve.

# Quinoa and Black Bean Salad

*Serves: 6*
*Ingredients:*

1 cup quinoa

1 cup black beans, cooked, rinsed and drained

½ cup sweet corn, cooked

1 red bell pepper, deseeded and chopped

4-5 spring onions, chopped

2 garlic cloves, crushed

1 tbsp dried mint

3 tbsp lemon juice

½ tsp salt

4 tbsp olive oil

*Directions:*

Rinse quinoa in a fine sieve under cold running water until water runs clear. Put quinoa in a pot with two cups of water. Bring to a boil, then reduce heat, cover and simmer for fifteen minutes or until water is absorbed and quinoa is tender. Fluff quinoa with a fork and set aside to cool.

Put beans, corn, bell pepper, spring onions and garlic in a salad bowl and toss to combine. Add quinoa and toss well again.

In a smaller bowl whisk together lemon juice, salt and olive oil and drizzle over the salad. Toss well and serve.

# Roasted Vegetable Quinoa Salad

*Serves: 6*
*Ingredients:*

2 zucchinis, peeled and cut into bite sized pieces

1 eggplant, peeled and cut into bite sized pieces

3 roasted red peppers, peeled cut into bite sized pieces

4-5 small white mushrooms, whole

1 cup quinoa

½ cup olive oil

2 tbsp apple cider vinegar

1 tsp summer savory

salt and pepper, to taste

*Directions:*

Toss the zucchinis, mushrooms and eggplant in half the olive oil, salt and black pepper. Place on a baking sheet in a single layer and bake in a preheated 350 F oven for 30 minutes flipping once.

Wash well, strain, and cook quinoa following package directions.

Prepare the dressing from the remaining olive oil, apple cider vinegar, summer savory, salt and black pepper. In a big bowl combine quinoa, roasted zucchinis, eggplant, mushrooms and roasted red peppers. Toss the dressing into the salad.

# Quinoa with Oven Roasted Tomatoes and Pesto

*Serves: 6*
*Ingredients :*

1 cup quinoa

2 cups water

1 cup cherry tomatoes, for roasting

½ cup cherry tomatoes, fresh

1 avocado, cut into chunks

½ cup black olives, pitted

**for the pesto**

2 cloves garlic, chopped

½ tsp salt

½ cup walnuts, toasted

1 cup basil leaves

1 tbsp lemon juice

4-6 tbsp olive oil

1 tsp summer savory

2 tbsp water (optional)

*Directions:*

Preheat the oven to 350 F and line a baking sheet with foil or baking paper. Wash and dry a cup of cherry tomatoes, arrange them on the baking sheet, drizzle with olive oil and savory and toss to coat well. Bake the tomatoes for about twenty minutes, flipping once, until they are brown. Sprinkle with salt.

Rinse quinoa very well in a fine mesh strainer under running water; set aside to drain. Place two cups of water and quinoa in a large saucepan over medium-high heat. Bring to the boil, then reduce heat to low. Simmer for fifteen minutes. Set quinoa aside, covered, for ten minutes and fluff with a fork.

Make the homemade pesto by placing garlic, walnuts and ½ teaspoon of salt in a food processor. Add basil and lemon juice and blend in batches until smooth. Add oil, one tablespoon at a time, processing in between, until the pesto is light and creamy. Taste for salt and add more if you like.

In a large mixing bowl, gently mix the quinoa with the tomatoes, avocado and olives. Spoon in the pesto and toss to distribute it evenly.

# Cucumber Quinoa Salad

*Serves: 6*
*Ingredients:*

1 cup quinoa

2 cups water

1 large cucumber, diced

½ cup black olives, pitted

2 tbsp lemon juice

2 tbsp olive oil

1 bunch fresh dill, finely cut

*Directions:*

Wash quinoa very well in a fine mesh strainer under running water and set aside to drain. Place quinoa and two cups of cold water in a saucepan over high heat and bring to the boil. Reduce heat to low and simmer for fifteen minutes. Set aside, covered, for ten minutes, then transfer to a large bowl.

Combine quinoa with the finely cut dill, diced cucumber and olives. Prepare a dressing from the lemon juice, olive oil, salt and pepper. Add it to the salad and toss to combine.

# Fresh Vegetable Quinoa Salad

*Serves: 6*
*Ingredients:*

1 cup quinoa

2 cups water

a bunch of green onions, chopped

2 green peppers, chopped

½ cup black olives, pitted and chopped

2 tomatoes, diced

1 cup sunflower seeds

3 tbsp olive oil

4 tbsp fresh lemon juice

1 tbsp dried mint

*Directions:*

Prepare the dressing by combining olive oil, lemon juice and dried mint in a small bowl and mixing it well. Place the dressing in the refrigerator until ready to use.

Wash well and cook quinoa according to package directions. When it is ready leave it aside for ten minutes, then transfer it to a large bowl. Add the diced peppers, finely cut green onions, olives and diced tomatoes, toss to combine.

Stir the dressing (it will have separated by this point) and add it to the salad, tossing to coat evenly. Add salt and pepper to taste and sprinkle with sunflower seeds.

# Warm Mushroom Quinoa Salad

*Serves: 4-5*
*Ingredients:*

1 cup quinoa

2 cups vegetable broth

1 tbsp olive oil

2-3 green onions, chopped

2 garlic cloves, chopped

10 white mushrooms, sliced

1-2 springs of fresh rosemary

½ cup sun-dried tomatoes, chopped

2 tbsp olive oil

salt and freshly ground black pepper

½ cup parsley, finely cut

*Directions:*

Wash well quinoa in plenty of cold water, strain it and put it in a saucepan. Add vegetable broth and bring to the boil. Lower heat and simmer for ten minutes until the broth is absorbed.

Heat oil in a frying pan and sauté onions for 2-3 minutes. Add garlic and sauté for another minute. Add sliced mushrooms and season with salt and pepper. Add the rosemary and cook the mushrooms until soft.

Combine quinoa with mushrooms and sun-dried tomatoes. Serve sprinkled with fresh parsley.

# Artichoke and Mushroom Salad

*Serves: 4-5*
*Ingredients:*

1 oz can artichoke hearts, drained, cut quartered

7-8 white button mushrooms, chopped

1 red pepper, chopped

1/3 cup chopped black olives

1 tbsp capers

3 tbsp lemon juice

2 tbsp olive oil

salt and pepper, to taste

*Directions:*

Place the artichokes and mushrooms in a large salad bowl and stir to mix well. Add in olives, capers and red pepper and toss to combine.

In a small bowl, whisk the lemon juice and olive oil until smooth. Pour over the salad, toss and serve.

# Quinoa and Asparagus Salad

*Serves: 6*
*Ingredients:*

1 cup quinoa

2 cups water

10-11 asparagus stalks, woody ends trimmed, cut

2 bell peppers, deseeded, chopped

¼ cup sunflower seeds

4 spring onions, chopped

2 tbsp fresh parsley, finely cut

2 tbsp lemon juice

1 tsp sugar

2 tbsp olive oil

1 tsp paprika

*Directions:*

Rinse quinoa very well in a fine mesh strainer under running water; set aside to drain. Place water and quinoa in a large saucepan over medium-high heat. Bring to the boil then reduce heat to low. Simmer for 15 minutes or until just tender. Set aside, covered, for 10 minutes.

Preheat an electric grill or grill pan and cook the asparagus for 2-3 minutes, or until tender crisp. Combine the asparagus, bell pepper, sunflower seeds, spring onions and parsley with the quinoa.

Whisk the lemon juice, sugar, oil and paprika in a small bowl until well combined. Add the dressing to the quinoa mixture. Season with black pepper and toss to combine.

# Warm Cauliflower and Quinoa Salad

*Serves: 4*
*Ingredients:*

1 small cauliflower, cut into florets

1 cup quinoa

2 cups water

1 tbsp paprika

salt, to taste

½ bunch spring onions, finely cut

5-6 tbsp olive oil

*Directions:*

Preheat oven to 350 F. Cut the cauliflower into bite sized pieces and place it in a roasting dish. Toss in olive oil, salt and paprika and roast, stirring occasionally until golden on the edges and soft.

Wash quinoa well and place in a medium saucepan with two cups of water. Simmer for 15 minutes then set aside for 3-4 minutes. Serve quinoa topped with cauliflower and sprinkled with spring onions.

# Quinoa, Zucchini and Carrot Salad

*Serves: 6*
*Ingredients:*

1 cup quinoa

2 cups water

2 big carrots, sliced lengthwise into thin ribbons

1 zucchini, sliced lengthwise into thin ribbons

1 big cucumber, sliced lengthwise into thin ribbons

*for the dressing:*

2 garlic cloves, minced

2 tbsp orange juice

1 tbsp apple cider vinegar

2 tbsp olive oil

black pepper, to taste

*Directions:*

Rinse the quinoa very well in a fine mesh strainer under running water; set aside to drain. Place water and quinoa in a large saucepan over medium-high heat. Bring to the boil then reduce heat to low. Simmer for 15 minutes or until just tender. Set aside, covered for 10 minutes.

Peel lengthwise the carrots and zucchini into thin ribbons. Steam them for 3-4 minutes. Peel the cucumber into ribbons too.

Prepare a dressing by mixing the orange juice, vinegar, olive oil and minced garlic.

Serve quinoa on each plate and arrange some of the vegetable stripes over it. Top with 2-3 tablespoons of the dressing.

# Tabbouleh

*Serves 6*
*Ingredients:*

1 cup raw bulgur

2 cups boiling water

a bunch of parsley, finely cut

2 tomatoes, chopped

3 tbsp olive oil

2 garlic cloves, minced

6-7 fresh onions, chopped

1 tbsp fresh mint leaves, chopped

juice of two lemons

salt and black pepper

Bring water and salt to a boil, then pour over bulgur. Cover and set aside for 15 minutes to steam. Drain excess water from bulgur and fluff with a fork. Leave to chill.

In a large bowl, mix together the parsley, tomatoes, olive oil, garlic, green onions and mint. Stir in the chilled bulgur and season to taste with salt, pepper and lemon juice.

# Fatoush

*Serves 6*
*Ingredients:*

2 cups lettuce, washed, dried, and chopped

3 tomatoes, chopped

1 cucumber, peeled and chopped

1 green pepper, seeded and chopped

½ cup radishes, sliced in half

1 small red onion, finely chopped

half a bunch of parsley, finely cut

2 tbsp finely chopped fresh mint

3 tbsp olive oil

4 tbsp lemon juice

salt and black pepper to taste

2 whole-wheat pita breads

Toast the pita breads in a skillet until they are browned and crisp. Set aside. Place the lettuce, tomatoes, cucumbers, green pepper, radishes, onion, parsley, and mint in a salad bowl. Break up the toasted pita into bite-size pieces and add to the salad.

Make the dressing by whisking together the olive oil with the lemon juice, a pinch of salt and some black pepper. Toss veggies together until everything is coated with dressing and serve.

# Greek Salad with Avocado

*Serves 6*
*Ingredients:*

2 cucumbers, diced

2 tomatoes, sliced

1 green lettuce, cut

2 red bell peppers, cut

½ cup olives, pitted

6 oz feta cheese, cubed

1 red onion, sliced

1 avocado, peeled and diced

2 tbsp olive oil

2 tbsp lemon juice

salt and ground black pepper

Dice the cucumbers and slice the tomatoes. Tear the lettuce or cut it in thin strips. De-seed and cut the peppers in strips. Dice the avocado. Mix all vegetables in a salad bowl.

Add the olives and the feta cheese cut in cubes. In a small cup, mix the olive oil and the lemon juice with salt and pepper. Pour over the salad and stir again.

# The Best Orzo Salad

*Serves 6*
*Ingredients:*

**For the dressing:**

1/3 cup extra-virgin olive oil

3/4 cup fresh lemon juice

1 tbsp dried mint

**For the salad:**

8 oz uncooked orzo

2 tbsp olive oil

a bunch of fresh onions, chopped

3 green peppers, diced

½ cup black olives, pitted, cut

2 tomatoes, diced

1 cup raw sunflower seeds

**The dressing:** Combine olive oil, lemon juice, and mint in a small bowl mixing well. Place the dressing in the refrigerator until ready to use.

Cook the orzo according to package directions (in salted water) and rinse thoroughly with cold water when you strain it. Transfer to a large bowl and toss with the olive oil. Allow orzo to cool completely.

Once orzo is cooled, add the diced peppers, finely cut fresh onions, olives and diced tomatoes stirring until mixed well.

Stir the dressing and add it to the salad, tossing to evenly coat. Add salt and pepper to taste and sprinkle with sunflower seeds.

# Heart Healthy Soups

# Mediterranean Chicken Soup

*Serves 6*
*Ingredients:*

about 1 lb chicken breasts

3-4 carrots, chopped

1 celery rib, chopped

1 red onion, chopped

1/3 cup rice

6 cups water

10 black olives, pitted and halved

fresh parsley or coriander, to serve

1/2 tsp salt

ground black pepper, to taste

lemon juice, to serve

*Directions:*

Place chicken breasts in a soup pot. Add onion, carrots, celery, salt, pepper and water. Stir well and bring to a boil.

Add rice, olives, stir and reduce heat. Simmer for 30-40 minutes.

Remove chicken from pot and let it cool slightly. Shred it and return it to pot. Serve soup with lemon juice and sprinkled with fresh parsley or coriander.

# Greek Lemon Chicken Soup

*Serves 6*
*Ingredients:*

12 oz uncooked boneless, skinless chicken breast, diced

1/3 cup rice

2 cups chicken broth

1 cup water

1 onion, finely diced

2 raw eggs

3 tbsp olive oil

1/2 cup fresh lemon juice

1 tablespoon salt

1 tsp ground pepper

a bunch of fresh parsley for garnish, finely cut

*Directions:*

In a medium pot, heat the olive oil and sauté the onions until they are soft and translucent. Add the chicken broth and water together with the washed rice and bring everything to a boil then reduce heat. When the rice is almost done, add the diced chicken breast to the pot. Let it cook for another 5 minutes or until the chicken is cooked through.

In a small bowl, beat the eggs and lemon juice together. Pour two cups of broth slowly into the egg mixture, whisking constantly. When all the broth is incorporated, add this mixture into the pot of chicken soup and stir well to blend. Do not boil any more.

Season with salt and pepper and garnish with parsley. Serve hot.

# Fresh Asparagus Soup

*Serves: 4*
*Ingredients:*

1 lb fresh asparagus, cut into pieces

1 small onion, chopped

3 garlic cloves, chopped

½ cup raw cashews, soaked in warm water for 1 hour

4 cups vegetable broth

2 tbsp olive oil

lemon juice, to taste

*Directions:*

Sauté onion for 3-4 minutes, stirring. Add in garlic and sauté for a minute more. Add in asparagus and sauté for 3-4 minutes.

Add broth, season with salt and pepper and bring to a boil then reduce heat and simmer for 20 minutes.

Set aside to cool, add cashews, and blend, until smooth. Season with lemon juice and serve.

# Creamy Red Lentil Soup

*Serves: 4*
*Ingredients:*

1 cup red lentils

1/2 small onion, chopped

1 garlic clove, chopped

1 red pepper, chopped

2 cups water

1 can coconut milk

3 tbsp olive oil

1 tsp paprika

1/2 tsp ginger

salt and black pepper, to taste

*Directions:*

Heat olive oil in a large saucepan and sauté onion, garlic, red pepper, paprika, ginger and cumin, stirring. Add in red lentils and water. Bring to a boil, cover, and simmer for 20 minutes.

Add in coconut milk and simmer for 5 more minutes. Remove from heat, season with salt and black pepper, and blend until smooth.

# Lentil, Barley and Kale Soup

*Serves: 4*
*Ingredients:*

2 medium leeks, chopped

2 garlic cloves, chopped

2 bay leaves

1 can tomatoes, diced and undrained

1/2 cup red lentils

1/2 cup barley

1 bunch kale, coarsely chopped

4 cups vegetable broth

3 tbsp olive oil

1 tbsp paprika

½ tsp cumin

*Directions:*

Heat olive oil in a large saucepan over medium-high heat and sauté leeks and garlic until fragrant. Add in cumin, paprika, tomatoes, lentils, barley and vegetable broth. Season with salt and pepper.

Cover and bring to a boil then reduce heat and simmer for 40 minutes or until barley is tender. Add in kale and let it simmer for a few minutes more until it wilts.

# Spinach and Mushrooms Soup

***Serves: 4-5***
***Ingredients:***

1 small onion, finely cut

1 small carrot, chopped

1 small zucchini, diced

1 medium potato, diced

6-7 white mushrooms, chopped

2 cups chopped fresh spinach

4 cups vegetable broth or water

4 tbsp olive oil

salt and black pepper, to taste

***Directions:***

Heat olive oil in a large pot over medium heat. Add potato, onion and mushroom and cook until vegetables are soft but not mushy.

Add chopped fresh spinach, zucchini and vegetable broth and simmer for about 20 minutes. Season to taste with salt and pepper.

# Broccoli and Potato Soup

***Serves: 4-5***
***Ingredients:***

1 lb broccoli, cut into florets

2 potatoes, chopped

1 onion, chopped

3 garlic cloves, crushed

4 cups water

2 tbsp olive oil

¼ tsp ground nutmeg

***Directions:***

Heat oil in a large saucepan over medium-high heat. Add onion and garlic and sauté, stirring, for 3 minutes, or until soft.

Add in broccoli, potato and 4 cups of cold water. Cover, bring to a boil, reduce heat and simmer, stirring, for 10-15 minutes, or until potatoes are tender.

Remove from heat and blend until smooth. Return to pan and cook until heated through. Season with nutmeg and black pepper before serving.

# Moroccan Lentil Soup

***Serves: 7-8***
***Ingredients:***

1 cup red lentils

1 cup canned chickpeas, drained

1 onion, chopped

2 cloves garlic, minced

1 cup canned tomatoes, chopped

1 cup canned white beans, drained

3 carrots, diced

1 celery rib, diced

5 cups water

3 tbsp olive oil

1 tsp ginger, grated

1 tsp ground cardamom

1/2 tsp cumin

***Directions:***

In a large pot, sauté onions, garlic and ginger in olive oil for about 5 minutes. Add the water, lentils, chickpeas, white beans, tomatoes, carrots, celery, cardamom and cumin.

Bring to a boil for a few minutes, then simmer for half an hour or longer until the lentils are tender. Puree half the soup in a food processor or blender. Return the pureed soup to the pot, stir and serve.

# Hearty Italian Minestrone

*Serves: 4-5*
*Ingredients:*

¼ head cabbage, chopped

2 carrots, chopped

1 celery rib, thinly sliced

1 small onion, chopped

2 garlic cloves, chopped

1 cup canned tomatoes, diced, undrained

1 cup fresh spinach, torn

1/2 cup pasta, cooked

3 cups water

2 tbsp olive oil

black pepper and salt, to taste

*Directions:*

Sauté the carrots, cabbage, celery, onion and garlic in oil for 5 minutes in a deep saucepan. Add water and tomatoes and bring to a boil.

Reduce heat and simmer uncovered, for 20 minutes, or until vegetables are tender. Stir in spinach, pasta, and season with pepper and salt to taste.

# Moroccan Chicken and Butternut Squash Soup

*Serves 7-8*
*Ingredients:*

3 skinless, boneless chicken thighs (about 14 oz), cut into bite-sized pieces

1 big onion, chopped

1 zucchini, quartered lengthwise and sliced into 1/2 inch pieces

3 cups peeled butternut squash, cut in 1/2 inch pieces

2 tbsp tomato paste

4 cups chicken broth

1/3 cup uncooked couscous

1/2 tsp ground cumin

1/4 teaspoon ground cinnamon

1 tsp paprika

1 tsp salt

2 tbsp fresh basil leaves, chopped

1 tbsp grated orange rind

3 tbsp olive oil

*Directions:*

Heat a soup pot over medium heat. Gently sauté onion, for 3-4 minutes, stirring occasionally. Add in chicken and cook for 4-5 minutes until chicken is brown on all sides. Add cumin, cinnamon and paprika and stir well.

Add butternut squash and tomato paste; stir again. Add in chicken broth and bring to a boil, then reduce heat and simmer for 10 minutes.

Stir in couscous, salt and zucchini pieces; cook until squash is tender. Remove pot from heat. Season with salt and pepper to taste. Stir in chopped basil and orange rind and serve.

# Chicken Soup with Vermicelli

*Serves 4*
*Ingredients:*

1 whole chicken leg or 1/2 lb chicken breast

1/2 cup vermicelli

1 carrot, grated

4 cups water

3 cloves of garlic, sliced

1 tsp salt

1/2 tsp black pepper

1 egg, beaten

2 tbsp lemon juice

*Directions:*

Place the chicken in a pot and add 4 cups of water. Add 1 tsp salt and boil until the chicken is cooked. Take the chicken out of the pot, let it cool a little and cut it into bite size pieces.

Add carrot and garlic to the soup and bring it to a boil. Add vermicelli and chicken pieces. Reduce heat and simmer over medium heat for 8-10 minutes. When ready, let it cool for a while.

Mix the beaten egg and lemon juice in a bowl and slowly stir into the soup. Do not boil it again. Serve soup warm, seasoned with black pepper to taste.

# French Vegetable Soup

*Serves: 6*
*Ingredients:*

1 leek, thinly sliced

1 large zucchini, peeled and diced

1 cup green beans, halved

2 garlic cloves, chopped

1 cup canned tomatoes, chopped

3.5 oz vermicelli, broken into small pieces

3 cups vegetable broth

3 tbsp olive oil

black pepper, to taste

*Directions:*

Sauté the leek, zucchini, green beans and garlic for about 5 minutes, stirring. Add in the vegetable broth and tomatoes and bring to a boil then reduce heat.

Add black pepper to taste and simmer for 10 minutes or until the vegetables are tender but still holding their shape. Stir in the vermicelli. Cover again and simmer for a further 5 minutes. Serve warm.

# Beetroot and Carrot Soup

*Serves: 5-6*
*Ingredients:*

4 beets, washed and peeled

2 carrots, peeled, chopped

2 potatoes, peeled, chopped

1 small onion, chopped

2 cups vegetable broth

2 cups water

3 tbsp olive oil

1 cup finely cut green onions, to serve

*Directions:*

Peel and chop the beets. Heat olive oil in a saucepan over medium-high heat and sauté the onion and carrot until tender. Add in beets, potatoes, broth and water. Bring to the boil then reduce heat and simmer, partially covered, for 30 minutes, or until beets are tender. Cool slightly.

Blend soup in batches until smooth. Return it to pan over low heat and cook, stirring, for 4-5 minutes, or until heated through. Season with salt and pepper. Serve sprinkled with green onions.

# Celery, Apple and Carrot Soup

*Serves: 4*
*Ingredients:*

2 celery ribs, chopped

1 large apple, chopped

1/2 small onion, chopped

3 carrots, chopped

2 garlic cloves, crushed

4 cups vegetable broth

3 tbsp olive oil

1 tsp ginger powder

salt and black pepper, to taste

*Directions:*

Heat olive oil over medium-high heat and sauté onion, garlic, celery and carrots for 3-4 minutes, stirring. Add in ginger, apple and vegetable broth.

Bring to a boil then reduce heat and simmer, covered, for 10 minutes. Blend until smooth and return to the pot. Cook over medium-high heat until heated through. Season with salt and pepper to taste and serve.

# Monastery Style White Bean Soup

*Serves: 6-7*
*Ingredients:*

2 cups white beans

2-3 carrots

1 large onion, finely chopped

1-2 tomatoes, grated

1 red bell pepper, chopped

1/2 cup finely cut fresh parsley

1 tbsp dried mint

1 tbsp paprika

¼ cup sunflower oil

salt, to taste

*Directions:*

Soak the beans in cold water for 3-4 hours or overnight, drain and discard the water.

Cover the beans with cold water. Add in oil, finely chopped carrots, onion and bell pepper.

Bring to a boil and simmer until the beans are tender. Add the grated tomatoes, mint, paprika and salt. Simmer for another 15 minutes. Serve sprinkled with finely chopped parsley.

# Fish and Noodle Soup

*Serves 4-5*
*Ingredients:*

14 oz firm white fish, cut into strips

2 carrots, cut into ribbons

1 zucchini, cut into thin ribbons

7 oz white button mushrooms, sliced

1 celery rib, finely cut

1 cup baby spinach

7 oz fresh noodles

3 cups chicken broth

2 cups water

2 tbsp soy sauce

1/2 tsp ground ginger

black pepper, to taste

*Directions:*

Place chicken broth, water and soy sauce in a large saucepan. Bring to a boil and add in carrots, celery, zucchini, mushrooms, ginger and noodles.

Cook, partially covered, for 3-4 minutes then add in fish and simmer for 3 minutes or until the fish is cooked through. Add baby spinach and simmer, stirring, for 1 minute, or until it wilts. Season with black pepper and serve.

# Hearty Lamb and Vegetable Soup

*Serves 6-7*
*Ingredients:*

2 cups roasted lamb, shredded

3 cups chicken or vegetable broth

1 cup water

1 cup canned tomatoes, diced, undrained

1 onion, chopped

1 large carrot, chopped

1 small turnip, chopped

1 celery rib

3 tbsp olive oil

salt and black pepper, to taste

*Directions:*

Gently heat olive oil in a large saucepan and sauté onion, carrot, celery and turnip, stirring, for 5 minutes, or until softened.

Add in lamb, broth, tomatoes, and a cup of water. Bring to the boil then reduce heat and simmer for 20 minutes, or until vegetables are tender. Season with salt and black pepper to taste.

# Creamy Cauliflower Soup

*Serves: 6-7*
*Ingredients:*

1 onion, finely cut

1 medium head cauliflower, chopped

2-3 garlic cloves, minced

½ cup raw cashews, soaked in warm water for 1 hour

3 cups vegetable broth

1 cup coconut milk

¼ cup olive oil

salt, to taste

black pepper, to taste

*Directions:*

Heat the olive oil in a large pot over medium heat and gently sauté the onion, cauliflower and garlic. Stir in the vegetable broth and bring the mixture to a boil.

Reduce heat, cover, and simmer for 30 minutes. Remove the soup from heat, add in cashews, coconut milk, and blend in a blender or with a hand mixer. Season with salt and pepper to taste.

# Pumpkin and Bell Pepper Soup

*Serves: 4*
*Ingredients:*

1 medium leek, chopped

9 oz pumpkin, peeled, deseeded, cut into small cubes

1/2 red bell pepper, cut into small pieces

1 can tomatoes, undrained, crushed

3 cups vegetable broth

1/2 tsp cumin

salt and black pepper, to taste

*Directions:*

Heat the olive oil in a medium saucepan and sauté the leek for 4-5 minutes. Add in the pumpkin and bell pepper and cook, stirring, for 5 minutes.

Add tomatoes, broth, and cumin and bring to a boil. Cover, reduce heat to low, and simmer, stirring occasionally, for 30 minutes or until vegetables are soft. Season with salt and pepper and leave aside to cool. Blend in batches and reheat to serve.

# Creamy Potato Soup

*Serves: 6-7*
*Ingredients:*

4-5 medium potatoes, peeled and diced

2 carrots, chopped

1 zucchini, chopped

1 celery rib, chopped

5 cups water

3 tbsp olive oil

½ tsp dried rosemary

salt and black pepper, to taste

1/2 cup fresh parsley, finely cut

*Directions:*

Heat olive oil over medium heat and sauté the vegetables for 2-3 minutes. Add 4 cups of water, rosemary and bring the soup to a boil, then lower heat and simmer until all the vegetables are tender.

Blend soup in a blender until smooth. Serve warm, seasoned with black pepper and parsley sprinkled over each serving.

# Shredded Cabbage Soup

***Serves: 4-5***
***Ingredients:***

1 onion, finely chopped

1 small cabbage, shredded

1 carrot, sliced

1 medium potato, peeled and diced

1 celery rib, sliced

2 tomatoes, diced

3 cups vegetable broth

3 tbsp sunflower oil

1 tsp cumin

salt, to taste

black pepper, to taste

***Directions:***

Heat sunflower oil over medium heat and gently sauté the onion for 2-3 minutes. Add in cabbage and sauté, stirring, for 2-3 minutes. Add carrots, potatoes, celery, tomatoes and cumin and stir again.

Add vegetable broth and bring the soup to a boil then reduce heat and simmer for 40 minutes. Season with salt and black pepper to taste.

# Easy Fish Soup

*Serves 6-7*
*Ingredients:*

1 lb white fish fillets cut in small pieces

9 oz scallops

1 onion, chopped

4 tomatoes, chopped

3 potatoes, diced

1 red pepper, chopped

2 carrots, diced

1 garlic clove, crushed

a bunch of fresh parsley

3 tbsp olive oil

a pinch of cayenne pepper

1 tsp dried oregano

1 tsp dried thyme

1 tsp dried dill

½ tsp pepper

½ cup white wine

4 cups water

1/3 cup heavy cream

*Directions:*

Heat the olive oil over medium heat and sauté the onion, red pepper, garlic and carrots until tender. Stir in the cayenne, herbs, salt, and pepper. Add the white wine, water, potatoes and tomatoes and bring to a boil.

Reduce heat, cover, and cook until the potatoes are almost done. Stir in the fish and the scallops and cook for another 10 minutes. Stir in the heavy cream and parsley and serve hot.

# Spanish Seafood Soup

***Serves 8-9***
***Ingredients:***

2 lb whole raw prawns

3 cups cold water

3 spring onions, chopped

1 bell pepper, finely chopped

2 large tomatoes, diced

1 tbsp tomato puree

2 garlic cloves, crushed

2 tbsp olive oil

2 bay leaves

1 tsp paprika

½ tsp cayenne pepper

salt and pepper, to taste

the juice of one small lemon

a bunch of parsley, chopped

***Directions:***

De-head and de-shell the prawns and leave them in a bowl to the side. Put the heads and shells in a pan with cold water. Add the bay leaves, bring to the boil and reduce heat. Simmer for 20 minutes.

While the broth is simmering sauté the shallots and pepper in olive oil for 5 minutes, then add the garlic for two more minutes. When the broth is ready strain it and add it to the the shallots.

Bring to the boil, add the tomatoes and tomato puree, the prawns, the mussels and simmer for 10 more minutes.

When the soup is ready, add the paprika and cayenne pepper, season to taste with salt and pepper and add the lemon juice. Garnish with parsley and serve.

# Hot Spanish Squid Soup

*Serves 4*
*Ingredients:*

1 lb squid, cleaned and cut into 1 inch pieces

2 garlic cloves; crushed

1/2 cup tomato puree or chopped tomatoes

3 cups water

1 tbsp olive oil

black pepper, to taste

1/2 cup parsley, finely chopped, to serve

*Directions:*

Heat olive oil in a soup pot over medium high heat and gently sauté garlic just for a minute. Add squid and sauté for 2-3 minutes, stirring. Add black pepper, tomato sauce or tomatoes and water.

Bring to a boil, then reduce heat and simmer for an hour. Serve sprinkled with parsley.

# Mediterranean Chickpea Soup

*Serves: 7-8*
*Ingredients:*

2 cups canned chickpeas, drained

1 onion, finely cut

2 cloves garlic, crushed

1 cup canned tomatoes, diced

6 cups vegetable broth

3 tbsp olive oil

1 bay leaf

½ tsp crushed rosemary

*Directions:*

Sauté onion and garlic in olive oil in a heavy soup pot. Add broth, chickpeas, tomato, bay leaf, and rosemary.

Bring to a boil then reduce heat and simmer for 30 minutes.

# Wild Mushroom Soup

*Serves: 4*
*Ingredients:*

1 lb mixed wild mushrooms

1 onion, chopped

2 garlic cloves, crushed

1 tsp dried thyme

3 cups vegetable broth

3 tbsp olive oil

salt and pepper, to taste

*Directions:*

Sauté onions and garlic in a large soup pot until transparent. Add thyme and mushrooms.

Stir and cook for 10 minutes, then add vegetable broth and simmer for another 10-20 minutes. Blend, season and serve.

# Thick Herb Soup

***Serves 4***
***Ingredients:***

3.5 oz parsley, finely cut

3.5 oz dill, finely cut

2 oz mint leaves, finely cut

2 oz celery leaves, finely cut

4 tbsp butter or olive oil

2 tbsp flour

3 cups water

½ cup thick yogurt or sour cream

juice of a lemon

2 egg yolks

1 tsp salt

***Directions:***

Wash the herbs, remove stalks and snip or chop finely. Heat butter or oil in a cooking pot, add prepared herbs, cover and simmer gently.

When the herbs are tender, add in the flour and stir to combine. Cook for a few moments before slowly adding the water, stirring all the time. Simmer for about 10-15 min.

Mix separately egg yolks, thick yogurt (or sour cream) and lemon juice. Add to the soup slowly, then stir well. The soup should not be allowed to boil any more.

# Spanish Gazpacho Soup

*Serves 6*
*Ingredients:*

2.25 lb tomatoes, peeled and halved

1 onion, sliced

1 green pepper, sliced

1 big cucumber, peeled and sliced

2 cloves garlic

1 tbsp red wine vinegar

salt, to taste

4 tbsp olive oil

**to garnish**

½ onion, chopped

1 green pepper, chopped

1 cucumber, chopped

*Directions:*

Place the tomatoes, garlic, onion, green pepper, cucumber, salt, olive oil and vinegar in a blender or food processor and puree until smooth, adding small amounts of cold water if needed to achieve desired consistency.

Serve the gazpacho chilled with the chopped onion, green pepper and cucumber sprinkled over each serving.

# Avocado Gazpacho

*Serves 4*
*Ingredients:*

2 ripe avocados, peeled, pitted and diced

1 cup tomatoes, diced

1 cup cucumbers, peeled and diced

1 small onion, chopped

10 oz chicken broth

2 tbsp lemon juice

1 tsp salt

black pepper, to taste

Place avocados, cucumbers, tomatoes, onion, broth, lemon juice and salt and pepper in a blender.

Blend until smooth and serve sprinkled with cilantro or parsley leaves.

# Cold Cucumber Soup

*Serves 4-5*
*Ingredients:*

1 large or two small cucumbers

2 cups yogurt

2-3 cloves garlic, crushed or chopped

1 cup cold water

4 tbsp sunflower or olive oil

2 bunches of fresh dill, finely chopped

1/2 cup crushed walnuts

Wash the cucumber, peel and cut into small cubes. In a large bowl dilute the yogurt with water to taste, add the cucumber and garlic stirring well.

Add salt to the taste, garnish with dill and the crushed walnuts and put in the fridge to cool.

# Spinach Soup

*Serves: 4*
*Ingredients:*

14 oz frozen spinach

1 large onion or 4-5 green onions

1 carrot, chopped

1/4 cup white rice

1-2 cloves garlic, cut

3 cups water

3-4 tbsp olive or sunflower oil

1 tsp paprika

black pepper, to taste

salt, to taste

*Directions:*

Heat oil in a cooking pot. Add the onion and carrot and sauté together for a few minutes, until just softened. Add chopped garlic, paprika and rice and stir for a minute. Remove from heat.

Add the spinach along with about 3 cups of hot water and season with salt and pepper. Bring back to the boil, then reduce the heat and simmer for around 30 minutes.

# Brussels Sprouts and Potato Soup

*Serves 4-5*
*Ingredients:*

16 oz Brussels sprouts

2 potatoes, peeled and chopped

1 onion, chopped

3 garlic cloves, crushed

4 cups water

2 tbsp olive oil

creme fraîche, to serve

salt and black pepper, to taste

*Directions:*

Heat oil in a large saucepan over medium-high heat. Add onion and garlic and sauté, stirring, for 1-2 minutes until fragrant.

Add in Brussels sprouts, potatoes, rosemary and 4 cups of vegetable broth.

Cover and bring to the boil, then reduce heat to low. Simmer for 30 minutes, or until potatoes are tender.

Remove from heat. Blend until smooth. Return to pan. Cook for 4-5 minutes or until heated through. Season with salt and pepper and serve with creme fraîche.

# Brussels Sprouts and Tomato Soup

*Serves 4-5*
*Ingredients:*

16 oz Brussels sprouts

4 large tomatoes, diced

1 medium onion, chopped

3 garlic cloves, crushed

1 tsp sugar

2 cups vegetable broth

1 tbsp paprika

2 tbsp olive oil

salt and black pepper, to taste

*Directions:*

Heat oil in a deep soup pot over medium-high heat. Add onion, garlic and paprika and sauté, stirring, for 2-3 minutes or until soft.

Add in tomatoes and vegetable broth. Cover and bring to the boil, then reduce heat to low and simmer, stirring, for 10 minutes.

Remove from heat and blend until smooth. Return to pan. Stir in Brussels sprouts. Cook for 15 minutes more. Season with salt and pepper before serving.

# Tomato and Quinoa Soup

*Serves: 4*
*Ingredients:*

4 cups chopped fresh tomatoes or 2 cups canned tomatoes

1 large onion, diced

1/3 cup quinoa, washed very well

3 cups water

2 garlic cloves, minced

3 tbsp olive oil

1 tsp salt

½ tsp black pepper

1 tsp sugar

1 cup finely cut fresh parsley

*Directions:*

Sauté onions and garlic in olive oil in a large soup pot. When onions have softened, add tomatoes and water and bring to a boil. Lower heat and simmer for 5 minutes.

Blend the soup then return to the pot. Stir in quinoa and sugar and bring to a boil again, then reduce heat and simmer 15 minutes, stirring occasionally. Sprinkle with parsley and serve.

# Spinach, Leek and Quinoa Soup

*Serves: 4-5*
*Ingredients:*

½ cup quinoa, very well washed

2 leeks halved lengthwise and sliced

1 onion, chopped

2 garlic cloves, chopped

1 can diced tomatoes, (15 oz), undrained

2 cups fresh spinach, cut

4 cups vegetable broth

2 tbsp olive oil

salt and pepper, to taste

*Directions:*

Heat olive oil in a large pot over medium heat and sauté onion for 2 minutes, stirring. Add leeks and cook for another 2-3 minutes, then add garlic and stir. Season with salt and black pepper to taste.

Add the vegetable broth, canned tomatoes and quinoa. Bring to a boil then reduce heat and simmer for 10 minutes. Stir in spinach and cook for another 5 minutes.

# Vegetable Quinoa Soup

*Serves: 6*
*Ingredients:*

½ cup quinoa

1/2 onion, chopped

1 potato, diced

1 carrot, diced

1 red bell pepper, chopped

2 tomatoes, chopped

1 small zucchini, peeled and diced

4 cups water

1 tsp dried oregano

3-4 tbsp olive oil

black pepper, to taste

2 tbsp fresh lemon juice

*Directions:*

Rinse quinoa very well in a fine mesh strainer under running water; set aside to drain.

Heat the oil in a large soup pot and gently sauté the onions and carrot for 2-3 minutes, stirring every now and then. Add in potato, bell pepper, tomatoes, spices and water. Stir to combine.

Cover, bring to a boil, then lower heat and simmer for 10 minutes. Add in the quinoa and the zucchini; cover and simmer for 15 minutes or until the vegetables are tender. Add in the lemon juice; stir to combine and serve.

# Heart Healthy Main Dish Recipes

# Mediterranean Chicken Casserole

*Serves 4*
*Ingredients:*

4 chicken breast halves

1 big onion, sliced

1 red bell pepper, thinly sliced

2 cups tomato pasta sauce

1/2 cup black olives, pitted

1/2 green olives, pitted

1/3 cup Parmesan cheese

¼ cup chopped parsley

3 tbsp olive oil

*Directions:*

Heat the oil in a large, deep frying pan over medium-high heat. Cook chicken breasts, turning, for 4-5 minutes or until golden. Transfer to a casserole.

Sauté the onion and bell pepper, stirring, for 3-4 minutes, or until the onion has softened. Transfer to the casserole. Add pasta sauce and olives. Season with salt and pepper. Bake in a preheated to 350 F for 30-35 minutes, stirring halfway through. Sprinkle with Parmesan cheese and parsley and bake for 3-4 minutes more.

# Chicken and Potato Casserole

*Serves 4*
*Ingredients:*

4 skinless, boneless chicken breast halves

12 oz baby potatoes

1 onion, sliced

2 carrots, halved

1 red bell pepper, halved, deseeded, cut

1 zucchini, peeled and sliced

4 garlic cloves, thinly sliced

1 cup water

3 tbsp olive oil

1 tsp dried oregano

**Directions:**

Preheat the oven to 350 F. Heat oil in a non stick frying pan over medium heat. Cook half the chicken, turning occasionally, for 5 minutes, or until brown all over. Set aside. Repeat with remaining chicken.

Peel the potatoes and cut into quarters, lengthwise. Peel and cut the carrots and the zucchini. Cut the onion and the pepper. Transfer chicken to an ovenproof dish and add the vegetables on and around the chicken. Add dried oregano, garlic, and water, distributing evenly across the pan.

Roast uncovered at 350 F for one hour. Halfway through stir gently. If needed, add a little more water.

# Easy Chicken Parmigiana

*Serves 4*
*Ingredients:*

4 chicken breast fillets

1 eggplant, peeled and sliced lengthwise

1 can tomatoes, diced

9 oz mozzarella cheese, sliced

2 tbsp olive oil

*Directions:*

In an ovenproof casserole, heat olive oil and brown the chicken pieces.

Place eggplant over the chicken and add in tomatoes. Top with mozzarella slices and bake in a preheated to 350 F for 20 minutes or until the cheese is golden.

# Mediterranean Chicken Drumstick Casserole

*Serves 4*
*Ingredients*

8 chicken drumsticks

1 leek, trimmed, thinly sliced

2 garlic cloves, crushed

1 cup canned tomatoes

1 tsp dried rosemary

1 cup canned chickpeas, drained and rinsed

cooked orzo or couscous, to serve

*Directions:*

Preheat the oven to 350 F. Heat the oil in a non stick frying pan over medium heat. Add half the chicken and cook, turning occasionally, for 5 minutes, or until brown all over. Transfer chicken to a big baking dish. Repeat with the remaining chicken.

Add leek and garlic to the pan and cook, stirring, for 3 minutes or until soft. Add tomatoes, chickpeas, thyme and rosemary and bring to the boil. Remove from heat. Pour over the chicken.

Cover and bake for 40 minutes or until chicken is tender. Season with salt and pepper. Serve with orzo or couscous.

# Mediterranean Lamb Casserole

*Serves 5*
*Ingredients:*

1 1/2 lb boned lean shoulder of lamb

3 onions, sliced

2 garlic cloves, chopped

1 cup canned chickpeas, drained and rinsed

2 zucchinis, cubed

1 cup cherry tomatoes, halved

1 cup beef broth

1 cup tomato juice

3 tbsp olive oil

1 tbsp flour

1 tbsp chopped fresh rosemary

1 tbsp fresh basil, chopped

1/3 tsp black pepper

½ cup fresh parsley leaves, to serve

*Directions:*

Cut the lamb into 1 inch cubes. In an ovenproof casserole, heat 2 tablespoons of the olive oil and gently sauté onions and garlic for about 2-3 minutes. Add the lamb and sauté, stirring, for about 4 minutes or until well browned on all sides. Add the flour and rosemary and stir.

Add the tomato juice and beef broth and bake in a preheated to 350 F for 1 hour. Stir in the chickpeas and bake for a further 1 hour or until the lamb is almost tender. Stir in courgettes, tomatoes, black pepper and basil. Cook for about 20 minutes longer or until the lamb is tender. Serve sprinkled with parsley.

# Lamb and Potato Casserole

*Serves 6*
*Ingredients:*

1 1/2 pounds shoulder lamb chops

12 small new potatoes, peeled, whole

3 large onions, sliced

2 carrots, sliced

2 tbsp olive oil

2 tsp dried parsley

2 tsp dried mint

1/2 tsp pepper

1/2 tsp salt

*Directions:*

Place lamb chops into a greased casserole dish. Cover them with sliced onion, carrots, parsley, salt and pepper. Arrange new potatoes on and around the meat. Add enough cold water to fill the dish halfway.

Bake, covered with foil, for 45 minutes in a preheated oven. Remove the foil and bake for 30 minutes more.

# Avocado and Rocket Pasta

*Serves: 4*
*Ingredients:*

3 cups cooked small pasta

½ cup cooked sweet corn

1 large avocado, peeled and diced

1 cup baby rocket leaves

5-6 fresh basil leaves, chopped

3 tbsp olive oil

3 tbsp lemon juice

*Directions:*

Whisk olive oil, lemon juice and basil in a small bowl. Season with salt and pepper to taste.

Combine pasta, avocado, corn and baby rocket. Add oil mixture and toss to combine.

# Delicious Broccoli Pasta

*Serves: 4*
*Ingredients:*

3 cups cooked small pasta

2 cups broccoli florets, cooked

1/3 cup walnuts, chopped

2 garlic cloves, chopped

10 cherry tomatoes, halved

5-6 fresh basil leaves

3 tbsp olive oil

3 tbsp lemon juice

*Directions:*

Combine olive oil, lemon juice, garlic, walnuts, basil and broccoli in blender. Season with salt and pepper to taste and blend until smooth.

Combine pasta, broccoli mixture and cherry tomatoes, toss, and serve.

# Creamy Butternut Squash Spaghetti

*Serves: 4*
*Ingredients:*

12 oz spaghetti

3 cups butternut squash, peeled, cut into small pieces

1/2 small onion, chopped

2 garlic cloves, chopped

1 carrot, cut

1 cup vegetable broth

5-6 fresh sage, chopped

1 tsp paprika

3 tbsp olive oil

salt and black pepper, to taste

*Directions:*

Heat olive oil in a large skillet and cook the onions, garlic and carrot until soft. Add the paprika and the pumpkin and mix well. Stir in vegetable broth and bring the mixture to a boil, then reduce heat and simmer until pumpkin is soft, about 15 to 20 minutes. Set aside to cool.

In a large pot of boiling salted water, cook spaghetti according to package instructions. Drain and set aside in a large bowl.

Once the pumpkin mixture has cooled, purée it until smooth, then season with salt and pepper to taste.

Combine spaghetti, pumpkin mixture and fresh sage leaves, toss, and serve.

# Sweet Potato Spaghetti

*Serves: 4*
*Ingredients:*

12 oz spaghetti

1 sweet potato peeled, slice into quarters

1/2 small onion, sliced

2 garlic cloves, chopped

1 carrot, quartered

1 large parsnip, quartered

1 tbsp tomato paste

1 tbsp rosemary, chopped

1/2 tsp thyme

4 tbsp olive oil

1 tbsp balsamic vinegar

salt and black pepper, to taste

1 cup finely gut green onions, to serve

*Directions:*

Arrange sweet potatoes, onion, carrot and parsnip on a lined baking sheet. Toss it in olive oil, salt, pepper and balsamic vinegar. Roast at 380 F until the vegetables are tender, about 20 minutes.

In a large pot of boiling salted water, cook spaghetti according to package instructions. Drain and set aside in a large bowl.

Once the vegetables have cooled, purée them together with tomato paste, thyme and rosemary. Add some water as needed to get the blade moving.

Combine spaghetti with the sauce. Add spaghetti water as needed to loosen. Sprinkle with chopped green onions and serve.

# Quick Orzo and Zucchini Dinner

*Serves: 4-5*
*Ingredients:*

1 cup orzo

2-3 medium zucchinis, peeled and cubed

1/2 onion

1/2 cup white wine

3 tbsp olive oil

1 tbsp dried oregano

1/3 cup fresh dill, finely cut

1 tsp salt

1 tsp fresh black pepper

2 tbsp lemon juice

*Directions:*

Cook the orzo according to package directions (in salted water) and rinse thoroughly with cold water when you strain it. Add in a tbsp of olive oil, stir, and set aside.

Gently sauté onion and zucchinis in 2 tbsp of olive oil, stirring, until onions are translucent. Add oregano and white wine and cook uncovered on low heat for 10 minutes. Add in orzo and stir to combine well. Add lemon juice, dill, and simmer, covered for 5 more minutes.

# Best Vegan Pizza

*Serves: 4*
*Ingredients:*

1 store-bought or homemade dough

1/3 cup onion, chopped

1 cup mushrooms, chopped

1/2 cup each red and green bell pepper, chopped

1/2 cup tomato sauce

1/2 cup vegan cheese

2 tbsp olive oil

1/2 tsp oregano

1 tsp dried basil

1/2 tsp garlic powder

salt and black pepper, to taste

*Directions:*

Heat a large skillet on medium heat and sauté the onion and peppers for 4-5 minutes until slightly charred. Add in the mushrooms, garlic powder, oregano and basil and sauté for 5 minutes more. Season with salt and black pepper to taste.

Roll out dough onto a floured surface and transfer to a parchment-lined 12 inch round baking sheet or pizza stone.

Top it with fresh or canned tomato sauce, vegan cheese and the sautéed vegetables.

Bake for 25-30 minutes in a preheated to 450 F oven or until the crust is golden brown and the sauce is bubbly. Let rest for 5 minutes before cutting, then serve immediately.

# Cheesy Potato and Zucchini Bake

*Serves 6*
*Ingredients:*

1 lb potatoes, peeled and sliced into rounds

3 zucchinis, sliced into rounds

1 can tomatoes, pureed

1 tsp Italian seasoning

1/2 cup grated Parmesan cheese

*Directions:*

Place the potatoes and zucchinis in a large, shallow ovenproof baking dish. Pour over the the pureed tomatoes. Sprinkle with the Italian seasoning and toss the everything together. Top with Parmesan cheese.

Bake in the preheated to 350 F oven for 40 minutes.

# Crispy Feta Cheese Pastry

*Serves 6*
*Ingredients:*

14 oz filo pastry

5 eggs

½ cup yogurt

8 oz feta cheese

3.5 oz butter

*Directions:*

Preheat the oven to 350 F. Combine the eggs, cheese and yogurt in a bowl. Melt the butter in a bowl.

Grease the base of a baking tray, at least 1.5 inch deep, with some of the butter. Take the filo sheets and lay them on a dry surface.

Place one sheet of filo pastry in the baking tray. Brush with melted butter using a pastry brush. Lay another sheet of pastry on top and brush with butter. Sprinkle some of the cheese mixture evenly over the butter-basted pastry. Continue alternating two sheets of butter-basted pastry with the cheese mixture. Repeat for 6 or 7 layers until all the sheets of pastry have been used up or the pie reaches the top of the baking tray, but make sure you finish with a sheet of pastry on top.

If there is any mixture left over brush the top of the Cheese Pastry in the tray, if there is none left - brush some butter.

Place the tray in the oven and bake for 20 minutes until slightly risen and golden. Serve warm.

# Pesto Chicken

*Serves 4*
*Ingredients:*

5-6 chicken breast halves

1 small jar pesto sauce

1 cup low fat sour cream

**Directions:**

In a bowl, combine pesto and sour cream.

Heat oven to 350 degrees F. Spray a casserole with non stick spray. Place chicken and pesto mixture into it, turn chicken to coat.

Bake for 35-40 minutes or until chicken juices run clear.

# Greek Chicken And Lemon Rice

*Serves 4*
*Ingredients:*

4 chicken thighs, skin on, bone in

1 small onion, finely cut

1 garlic clove, minced

1 cup white rice

1 1/2 cups water

3 tbsp olive oil

1 tsp salt

black pepper, to taste

*for the marinade:*

2 lemons, juiced

2 tbsp lemon zest

1 tbsp dried oregano

4 garlic cloves, minced

1 tsp salt

*Directions:*

Combine the chicken and marinade ingredients in a bowl and set aside for at least 30 minutes.

Heat olive oil in an ovenproof casserole dish on medium-high heat. Remove chicken from marinade, but reserve the marinade. Cook chicken pieces for a few minutes on each side, enough to seal them.

Add in onions, garlic, rice and reserved marinade and stir to combine.

Stir in water, season with salt and pepper to taste, and bake in a preheated to 350 F oven for 30-35 minutes or until the rice and chicken are done.

# Spicy Chicken and Bean Stew

***Serves 4***
***Ingredients:***

2 chicken breasts, cut in cubes

1 small onion, finely cut

1 garlic clove, minced

2 red chillies, deseeded and chopped

1 can tomatoes, diced and undrained

2 cans kidney beans, drained

1 cup hot chicken broth

3 tbsp olive oil

1 tsp hot paprika

1 tsp salt

black pepper, to taste

1/2 cup fresh parsley, finely cut, to serve

1 cup sour cream

***Directions:***

Heat the olive oil in an ovenproof casserole dish on medium-high heat. Cook chicken for a few minutes on each side, until brown all over.

Add in onions, garlic, chillies and hot paprika and stir to combine.

Stir in chicken broth, beans and tomatoes, season with salt and pepper to taste, cover, and cook until the chicken is cooked through and tender.

Stir through the parsley and serve with sour cream.

# Mushroom and Spinach Scrambled Eggs

*Serves 5-6*
*Ingredients:*

1 small onion, finely chopped

3 cups white mushrooms, thinly sliced

4 cups baby spinach, torn

8 eggs

2 tbsp olive oil

*Directions:*

In a large pan, sauté onion and mushrooms in oil, over medium heat, until soft, about 7 min.

Add the spinach and stir until wilted. Season with salt and pepper to taste.

Add in the eggs, stir, and cook until the eggs are softly set. Serve and enjoy!

# Feta and Olive Scrambled Eggs

*Serves 4*
*Ingredients:*

5-6 green onions, finely cut

10 oz feta cheese, crumbled

1 cup black olives, pitted and halved

8 eggs

2 tbsp olive oil

*Directions:*

In a large pan, sauté the onions in olive oil, over medium heat, until soft, about 1-2 min.

Add the cheese and all eggs, stir, and cook until well mixed and not too liquid.

Stir in the olives, cook for a minute more, and serve.

# Spinach Omelet

*Serves 4*
*Ingredients:*

1 cup fresh spinach, chopped

5 green onions, chopped

1/2 cup cherry tomatoes, halved

3 eggs, gently beaten

3 tbsp olive oil

*Directions:*

Heat the olive oil in a large skillet. Gently sauté the chopped vegetables.

Beat the eggs with salt and black pepper in a bowl. Pour them over the vegetables and cook until firm. Flip omelet and cook the other side.

# Greek Chicken Casserole

*Serves 4*
*Ingredients:*

4 skinless, boneless chicken breast halves or 8 tights

2 lb potatoes, cubed

1/2 lb green beans, trimmed and cut in 1 inch pieces

1 big onion, chopped

2 cups diced, canned tomatoes, undrained

5 cloves garlic, minced

1/4 cup water

1/2 cup feta cheese, crumbled

salt and black pepper, to taste

*Directions:*

Preheat oven to 350 F. Heat oil in a large baking dish over medium heat. Add onion and sauté for 2 minutes. Add thyme, black pepper and garlic and sauté for another minute. Add potatoes and sauté, for 2-3 minutes, or until they begin to brown. Stir in beans, water and tomatoes.

Remove from heat. Arrange chicken pieces into the vegetables, sprinkle with salt and pepper and top with feta. Cover and bake for 40 minutes, stirring gently halfway through. Serve the vegetable mixture on a plate underneath or beside the chicken.

# Hunter Style Chicken

*Serves 4-6*
*Ingredients:*

1 chicken (3-4 lbs), cut into pieces

2 medium onions, thinly sliced

1 red bell pepper, cut

6-7 white mushrooms, sliced

2 cups canned tomatoes, diced and drained

3 garlic cloves, thinly sliced

2 tbsp olive oil

salt and freshly ground pepper

1/3 cup white wine

1/2 cup parsley leaves, finely cut

1 tsp sugar

*Directions:*

Rinse chicken pieces and pat dry. Heat olive oil in a large skillet on medium-high heat. Working in batches cook the chicken pieces until nicely browned, 5-6 minutes each side.

Transfer chicken to an ovenproof dish and set aside. In the same skillet, sauté the sliced onions and bell pepper for a few minutes. Add the mushrooms and cook some more until onion is translucent. Add garlic and cook a minute more.

Transfer vegetable mixture to the baking dish and add in wine, tomatoes and a teaspoon of sugar. Stir and bake for 40 minutes or until chicken is tender. Sprinkle with parsley, set aside for 3-4 minutes and serve.

# Sweet and Sour Sicilian Chicken

*Serves 4*
*Ingredients:*

4 chicken thigh fillets

1 large red onion, sliced

3 garlic cloves, chopped

2 tbsp flour

1/3 cup dry white wine

1 cup chicken broth

1/2 cup green olives

2 tbsp olive oil

2 bay leaves

1 tbsp fresh oregano leaves

2 tbsp brown sugar or honey

2 tbsp red wine vinegar

salt and black pepper, to taste

*Directions:*

Combine the flour with salt and black pepper and coat well all chicken pieces. Heat oil in ovenproof casserole and cook the chicken in batches, for 1-2 minutes each side, or until golden.

Add in onion, garlic, and wine and cook, stirring for 1 more minute. Add the chicken broth, olives, bay leaves, oregano, sugar and vinegar and bake, in a preheated to 380 F oven, for 20 minutes, or until the chicken is cooked through.

# Moroccan Chicken Casserole

*Serves 4-5*
*Ingredients:*

1 whole chicken (3-4 lbs), cut into pieces

2 large onions, grated

2 or 3 cloves of garlic, finely chopped or pressed

1 tsp ginger

1 tsp cumin

1 tsp paprika

1 tsp black pepper

1 tsp turmeric

1/2 teaspoon salt

1/2 cup green or black olives, or mixed

1 preserved lemon, quartered and deseeded

5 tbsp olive oil

one bunch of fresh coriander

one bunch of fresh parsley

*Directions:*

Rinse and dry chicken and place onto a clean plate.

In a large bowl, mix three tablespoons of olive oil, salt, half the onions, garlic, ginger, cumin, paprika, and turmeric. Mix thoroughly, crush the garlic with your fingers, and add a little water to make a paste. Roll the chicken pieces into that marinade and leave for 10 to 15 minutes.

Heat an ovenproof dish on medium heat and add 2 tablespoons of olive oil. Add in the chicken and marinade juices together with the remaining onions, olives and chopped preserved lemon.

Tie the parsley and coriander together into a bouquet and place on top of the chicken. Bake in a preheated to 350 F oven for 45 minutes or until the chicken is cooked through and quite tender. Serve with couscous, rice or rice pilaf.

# Chicken Moussaka

*Serves 6*
*Ingredients:*

2 big eggplants, cut into 1/2 inch thick rounds

olive oil cooking spray

1 tbsp salt

1 big onion, chopped

1/2 tsp ground cinnamon

1/2 tsp ground nutmeg

1/4 tsp ground coriander

1/4 tsp ground ginger

2 cups canned tomatoes, undrained, chopped

2 cups skinless, shredded, roast chicken

1/2 cup finely chopped fresh parsley leaves

1 tsp sugar

1 cup yogurt

1 cup Parmesan cheese

salt and black pepper to taste

*Directions:*

Place eggplant slices on a tray and sprinkle with plenty of salt. Let sit for 30 minutes, then rinse with cold water. Lay slices out flat and use a clean kitchen towel to squeeze out excess water and pat dry.

Heat a frying pan over medium high heat. Spray both sides of eggplant with oil. Cook in batches for 3 to 4 minutes each side or until golden. Transfer to a plate.

In the same pan sauté onion, stirring, for 3 to 4 minutes or until softened. Add spice. Sauté for one minute until fragrant. Add tomatoes and sugar, stir and sauté until thickened. Add chicken and parsley and stir well to combine.

Arrange half the eggplant slices in a casserole. Cover with chicken and tomato mixture and arrange remaining eggplant. Top with yogurt and sprinkle with Parmesan cheese. Bake for 30 minutes or until golden. Set aside for five minutes and serve.

# Eggplant and Chickpea Stew

*Serves: 4*
*Ingredients:*

2-3 eggplants, peeled and diced

1 onion, chopped

2-3 garlic cloves, crushed

8 oz can chickpeas, drained

8 oz can tomatoes, undrained, diced

1 tbsp paprika

1/2 tsp cinnamon

1 tsp cumin

3 tbsp olive oil

salt and pepper, to taste

*Directions:*

Peel and dice the eggplants. Heat olive oil in a large deep frying pan and sauté onions and crushed garlic. Add in paprika, cumin and cinnamon. Stir well to coat evenly. Sauté for 3-4 minutes until the onions have softened.

Add in the eggplant, tomatoes and chickpeas. Bring to a boil, lower heat and simmer, covered, for 15 minutes, or until the eggplant is tender.

Uncover and simmer for a few more minutes until the liquid evaporates.

# Green Pea and Mushroom Stew

*Serves: 4*
*Ingredients:*

1 cup green peas (fresh or frozen)

4 large mushrooms, sliced

3 green onions, chopped

1-2 cloves garlic

4 tbsp olive oil

1/2 cup water

1/2 cup finely chopped dill

salt and black pepper, to taste

*Directions:*

In a saucepan, sauté mushrooms, green onions and garlic. Add in the green peas and simmer for 10 minutes until tender.

When ready sprinkle with dill and serve.

# Tomato Leek Stew

***Serves: 5-6***
***Ingredients:***

1 lb leeks, cut into rings

1/2 cup vegetable broth

2 tbsp tomato paste

4 tbsp olive oil

1 tbsp dried mint

salt to taste

fresh ground pepper to taste

***Directions:***

Heat the oil in a heavy wide saucepan or sauté pan. Add in leeks, salt, pepper, and sauté, stirring, for 5 minutes. Add in vegetable broth and bring to a boil.

Cover and simmer over low heat, stirring often, for about 10-15 minutes or until leeks are tender. Gently stir in tomato paste and dried mint, raise heat to medium, uncover and simmer for 5 minutes.

# Potato and Leek Stew

*Serves: 4*
*Ingredients:*

12 oz potatoes, diced

2-3 leeks cut into thick rings

5-6 tbsp olive oil

1 cup water

1/2 cup finely cut parsley

1 tsp paprika

salt and black pepper, to taste

*Directions:*

Heat olive oil in a heavy wide saucepan or sauté pan. Add in leeks, paprika, salt and pepper, and sauté for 2-3 minutes, stirring. Add in potatoes and water. The water should cover the vegetables.

Bring to a boil and simmer until vegetables are tender. Sprinkle with finely chopped parsley and serve.

# Spinach with Rice

*Serves: 4*
*Ingredients:*

1.5 lb fresh spinach, washed, drained and chopped

1/2 cup rice

1 onion, chopped

1 carrot, grated

5 tbsp olive oil

2 cups water

*Directions:*

Heat the oil in a large skillet and cook the onions until soft. Add paprika, carrot and rice and stir. Add two cups of warm water stirring constantly as the rice absorbs it, and simmer for 10 minutes.

Wash the spinach cut it in strips then add to the rice and cook until it wilts. Remove from heat and season to taste.

# Rich Vegetable Stew

*Serves: 6*
*Ingredients:*

3-4 potatoes, peeled and diced

2 tomatoes, diced

2 carrots, chopped

1 onion, finely chopped

1 zucchini, peeled and cut

1 eggplant, peeled and cut

1 celery rib, chopped

1/2 cup green peas, frozen

1/2 green beans, frozen

3 tbsp olive oil

1 bunch of parsley

1 tsp black pepper

1 tsp salt

*Directions:*

In a deep saucepan, sauté the finely chopped onion, carrots and celery in a little oil. Add in green peas, the green beans, black pepper and stir well. Pour over 1 cup of water, cover and let simmer.

After 15 minutes add the diced potatoes, the zucchini, the eggplant and the tomato.

Transfer everything into an ovenproof baking dish, sprinkle with parsley and bake for about 30 minutes at 350 F.

# Hearty Baked Beans

*Serves: 8-10*
*Ingredients:*

1 1/2 dried white beans

2 medium onions

1 red bell pepper, chopped

1 carrot, chopped

1/4 cup olive oil

1 tsp paprika

1 tsp black pepper

1 tbsp plain flour

½ bunch fresh parsley and mint

1 tsp salt

*Directions:*

Wash the beans and soak them in water overnight. In the morning discard the water, pour enough cold water to cover the beans, add one of the onions, peeled but left whole. Cook until the beans are soft but not falling apart. If there is too much water left, drain the beans.

Chop the other onion and fry it a frying pan along with the chopped bell pepper and the carrot. Add in paprika, plain flour and the beans.

Stir well and pour the mixture in a baking dish along with some parsley, mint, and salt. Bake in a preheated to 350 F oven for 20 minutes. The beans should not be too dry. Serve warm.

# Rice Stuffed Bell Peppers

*Serves: 4-5*
*Ingredients:*

8 bell peppers, cored and seeded

1 1/2 cups rice

2 onions, chopped

1 tomato, chopped

1/2 cup fresh parsley, chopped

3 tbsp olive oil

1 tbsp paprika

*Directions:*

Heat the olive oil and sauté the onions for 2-3 minutes. Add in paprika, rice, diced tomato and season with salt and pepper. Add ½ cup of hot water and cook the rice, stirring, until the water is absorbed.

Stuff each pepper with rice mixture using a spoon. Every pepper should be ¾ full. Arrange the peppers in a deep ovenproof dish and top up with warm water to half fill the dish.

Cover and bake for about 20 minutes at 350 F. Uncover and cook for another 15 minutes until the peppers are well cooked through.

# Bell Peppers Stuffed with Beans

*Serves: 5*
*Ingredients:*

10 dried red bell peppers

1 cup dried white beans

1 onion, finely cut

3 cloves garlic, chopped

2 tbsp flour

1 carrot, chopped

1 cup fresh parsley, finely cut

1/2 cup crushed walnuts

1 tsp paprika

salt

*Directions:*

Put the dried peppers in warm water and leave them for 1 hour.

Cook the beans. Gently sauté onion and carrot and combine with the cooked beans. Add in the finely chopped parsley and walnuts. Stir.

Drain the peppers, then fill them with the bean mixture and arrange in a baking dish, covering the openings with flour to seal them during the baking. Bake for about 30 minutes at 350 F

# Stuffed Grapevine Leaves

*Serves: 6*
*Ingredients:*

1.5 oz grapevine leaves, canned

2 cups rice

2 onions, chopped

2-3 cloves garlic, chopped

1/2 cup of currants

1/2 cup fresh parsley, finely cut

1/2 cup fresh dill, finely cut

1 lemon, juice only

1 tsp dried mint

1 tsp salt

1 tsp black pepper

6 tbsp virgin olive oil

*Directions:*

Heat 3 tablespoons of olive oil in a frying pan and sauté the onions and garlic until golden. Add the washed and drained rice, the currants, dill and parsley and sauté, stirring. Add in lemon juice, black pepper, dried mint and salt.

Place a grapevine leaf on a chopping board, with the stalk towards you and the vein side up. Place about 1 teaspoon of the filling in the center of the leaf and towards the bottom edge. Fold the bottom part of the leaf over the filling, then draw the sides in and towards the middle, rolling the leaf up. The vine leaves should be well tucked in, forming a neat parcel. The stuffing should feel compact and evenly distributed.

Cover the bottom of a pot with grapevine leaves and arrange the stuffed vine leaves, packing them tightly together, on top. Pour in some water, to just below the level of the stuffed leaves. Place a small, flat ovenproof plate upside down on top, in order to prevent scattering.

Cover with a lid, bring to a boil, then reduce heat and simmer for about an hour checking occasionally that the bottom of the pot does not burn. Serve warm or cold.

# Stuffed Cabbage Leaves

*Serves: 8*
*Ingredients:*

20-30 pickled cabbage leaves

1 onion, finely cut

2 leeks, chopped

1 1/2 cup white rice

1/2 cup currants

1/2 cup almonds, blanched, peeled, and chopped

2 tsp paprika

1 tbsp dried mint

1/2 tsp black pepper

½ cup olive oil

salt, to taste

*Directions:*

Sauté the onion and leeks in olive oil for about 2-3 minutes. Stir in paprika, black pepper and rice and continue sautéing until the rice is translucent. Remove from heat and add the currants, finely chopped almonds and the peppermint. Add salt only if the cabbage leaves are not too salty.

In a large pot, place a few cabbage leaves on the base. Place a cabbage leaf on a large plate with the thickest part closest to you. Spoon 1-2 teaspoons of the rice mixture and fold over each edge to create a tight sausage-like parcel. Place in the pot, making two or three layers.

Cover with a few cabbage leaves and pour over some boiling

water so that the water level remains lower than the top layer of cabbage leaves. Top with a small plate upside down to prevent scattering.

Bring to the boil then lower the heat and cook for around 40 minutes. Serve warm or at room temperature.

# Green Bean and Potato Stew

*Serves: 5-6*
*Ingredients:*

2 cups green beans, fresh or frozen

2 onions, chopped

3-4 potatoes, peeled and diced

2 carrots, cut

4 cloves garlic, crushed

1 cup fresh parsley, chopped

1/2 cup fresh dill, finely chopped

4 tbsp olive oil

1/2 cup water

2 tsp tomato paste

salt and pepper, to taste

*Directions:*

Heat olive oil in a deep saucepan and gently sauté the onions and garlic. Add in green beans and the remaining ingredients.

Cover, and simmer over medium heat for about an hour or until all vegetables are tender. Check after 30 minutes; add more water if necessary. Serve sprinkled with fresh dill.

# Cabbage and Rice Stew

*Serves: 4*
*Ingredients:*

1 cup long grain white rice

2 cups water

2 tbsp olive oil

1 small onion, chopped

1 clove garlic, crushed

1/4 head cabbage, cored and shredded

2 tomatoes, diced

1 tbsp paprika

1/2 cup parsley, finely cut

salt and black pepper, to taste

*Directions:*

Heat the olive oil in a large pot. Add in onion and garlic and cook until transparent. Add paprika, rice and water, stir, and bring to boil. Simmer for 10 minutes.

Add in cabbage, tomatoes, and cook for about 20 minutes, stirring occasionally, until the cabbage cooks down. Season with salt and pepper and serve sprinkled with parsley.

# Rice with Leeks and Olives

*Serves: 4-6*
*Ingredients:*

6 large leeks, cleaned and sliced into bite sized pieces (about 6-7 cups of sliced leeks)

1 large onion, cut

20 black olives pitted, chopped

1/2 cup hot water

1/4 cup olive oil

1 cup rice

2 cups boiling water

black pepper, to taste

*Directions:*

In a large saucepan, sauté the leeks and onion in olive oil for 4-5 minutes. Cut and add the olives and 1/2 cup of water. Bring temperature down, cover saucepan, and cook for 5 minutes, stirring occasionally.

Add in rice and 2 cups of hot water, bring to a boil, cover, and simmer for 15 more minutes, stirring occasionally. Remove from heat and allow to 'sit' for 30 minutes before serving so that the rice can absorb any liquid left.

# Rice and Tomato Stew

*Serves: 6-7*
*Ingredients:*

1 cup rice

1 big onion, chopped

2 cups canned tomatoes, diced or 5 big ripe tomatoes

1 tbsp paprika

1/4 cup olive oil

1 tsp savory

½ cup fresh parsley, finely cut

1 tsp sugar

*Directions:*

Wash and drain the rice. In a large saucepan, sauté the onion in olive oil for 4-5 minutes. Add in paprika and rice, stirring constantly, until the rice becomes transparent.

Stir in 2 cups of hot water and the tomatoes. Mix well and season with salt, pepper, savory and a tsp of sugar to neutralize the acidic taste of the tomatoes. Simmer over medium heath for about 20 minutes. When ready sprinkle with parsley.

# Roasted Cauliflower

*Serves: 4*
*Ingredients:*

1 medium cauliflower, cut into florets

4 garlic cloves, lightly crushed

1 tsp fresh rosemary

salt and black pepper, to taste

1/4 cup olive oil

*Directions:*

Mix olive oil oil, rosemary, salt, pepper and garlic together. Toss in cauliflower and place in a baking dish in one layer.

Roast in a preheated to 350 F oven for 20 minutes; stir and bake for 10 more minutes.

# New Potatoes with Herbs

*Serves: 4-5*
*Ingredients:*

2 lbs small new potatoes

5 tbsp olive oil

1 tbsp dried mint

1 tbsp finely chopped parsley

1 tbsp rosemary

1 tbsp oregano

1 tbsp dill

1 tsp salt

1 tsp black pepper

*Directions:*

Wash the young potatoes, cut them in halves if too big, and them in a baking dish.

Pour the olive oil over the potatoes. Season with the herbs, salt and pepper and toss to coat evenly. Bake for 30-40 minutes at 350 F.

# Potato and Zucchini Bake

*Serves: 6*
*Ingredients:*

1½ lb potatoes, peeled and sliced into rounds

5 zucchinis, peeled and sliced into rounds

2 onions, sliced

3 tomatoes, pureed

½ cup water

4 tbsp olive oil

1 tsp dried oregano

1/3 cup fresh parsley leaves, chopped

salt and black pepper, to taste

*Directions:*

Place potatoes, zucchinis and onions in a large, shallow ovenproof baking dish.

Pour over the the olive oil and pureed tomatoes. Add salt and freshly ground pepper to taste and toss the everything together. Add in water.

Bake in a preheated to 350 F oven for an hour, stirring halfway through.

# Baked Mediterranean Casserole with Tofu and Feta Cheese

*Serves 4-5*
*Ingredients:*

2 lbs small new potatoes, washed and halved

1/2 cup feta cheese, crumbled

1 cup spicy tofu pieces

3 cloves garlic, crushed

2 cups cherry or grape tomatoes

3 tbsp rosemary, chopped or minced

3 tbsp olive oil

1/2 cup Parmesan cheese

salt and pepper to taste

*Directions:*

Preheat the oven to 350 F. Put the sliced potatoes, garlic, olive oil, rosemary, salt and pepper in an oven proof baking dish and mix them all together well so that the potatoes are well coated.

Place in the oven and bake for 20 minutes then stir and add the tomatoes, tofu and feta cheese. Sprinkle with Parmesan cheese and cook for 15 minutes more.

# Okra and Tomato Casserole

*Serves: 4-5*
*Ingredients:*

1 lb okra, stem ends trimmed

4 large tomatoes, cut into wedges

3 garlic cloves, chopped

3 tbsp olive oil

1 tsp salt

black pepper, to taste

*Directions:*

In a large casserole, mix together trimmed okra, sliced tomatoes, olive oil and chopped garlic. Add salt and pepper and toss to combine. Bake in a preheated to 350 F oven for 45 minutes, or until the okra is tender.

# Roasted Cauliflower

*Serves: 4*
*Ingredients:*

1 medium cauliflower, cut into florets

4 garlic cloves, lightly crushed

1 tsp fresh rosemary

salt and black pepper, to taste

1/4 cup olive oil

*Directions:*

Mix olive oil oil, rosemary, salt, pepper and garlic together. Toss in cauliflower and place in a baking dish in one layer.

Roast in a preheated to 350 F oven for 20 minutes; stir and bake for 10 more minutes.

# Roasted Brussels Sprouts

*Serves: 4-5*
*Ingredients:*

1 ½ lb Brussels sprouts, rinsed

1 tbsp summer savory

3 tbsp olive oil

3 tbsp balsamic vinegar

salt and black pepper, to taste

*Directions:*

Preheat the oven to 400 F. Place whole sprouts in a bowl. (If they are too large-cut in half). Add olive oil, balsamic vinegar and and summer savory and toss to coat evenly.

Season with salt and pepper. Place Brussels sprouts on a baking sheet and roast for 35 minutes, stirring a couple of times, or until tender. Serve warm.

# Roasted Butternut Squash

*Serves: 4*
*Ingredients:*

½ butternut squash, peeled, seeds removed, flesh chopped

2 garlic cloves, finely chopped

2 sprigs fresh rosemary, leaves only

3-4 tbsp olive oil

salt and black pepper, to taste

*Directions:*

Preheat the oven to 350 F. Place the butternut squash pieces onto a baking tray and scatter over the rosemary and the chopped garlic.

Drizzle with olive oil and season, to taste, with salt and freshly ground black pepper. Transfer to the oven and roast for 12-15 minutes, or until the squash is tender and golden-brown.

# Roasted Artichoke Hearts

*Serves: 4*
*Ingredients:*

2 cans artichoke hearts

4 garlic cloves, quartered

2 tbsp olive oil

1 tsp summer savory

salt and pepper, to taste

2-3 tbsp lemon juice, to serve

*Directions:*

Preheat oven to 350 F. Drain artichoke hearts and rinse them well. Place them in a bowl and toss in garlic, savory and olive oil.

Arrange artichoke hearts in a baking dish and bake for about 45 minutes tossing a few times if desired. Season with salt and pepper, and serve with lemon juice.

# Beet Fries

*Serves: 4*
*Ingredients:*

3 beets, cut in strips

3 tbsp olive oil

1 cup finely cut spring onions

2 garlic cloves, crushed

1 tsp salt

*Directions:*

Line a baking dish with baking paper. Wash and peel the beets then cut them in strips similar to French fries. Toss the beets with olive oil, spring onions, garlic and salt.

Arrange the beets on a prepared baking sheet and place it in a preheated to 425 F oven for 25-30 minutes, flipping halfway through.

# Grilled Vegetable Skewers

*Serves: 4*
*Ingredients:*

1 red pepper

1 green pepper

3 zucchinis, halved lengthwise and sliced

3 onions, quartered

12 medium mushrooms, whole

2 garlic cloves, crushed

2 tbsp olive oil

1 tsp summer savory

1 tsp cumin

1 spring fresh rosemary, leaves only

salt and ground black pepper, to taste

*Directions:*

Deseed and cut the peppers into chunks. Divide between 6 skewers threading alternately with the zucchinis, onions and mushrooms. Set aside the skewers in a shallow plate.

Mix the crushed garlic with the herbs, cumin, salt, black pepper and olive oil. Roll each skewer in the mixture. Bake them on a hot barbecue or char grill, turning occasionally, until slightly charred.

# Heart Healthy Breakfasts and Desserts

# Raisin Quinoa Breakfast

*Serves: 2*
*Ingredients:*

½ cup quinoa

1 cup water

1 tbsp brown sugar

1 tsp cinnamon

½ tsp vanilla

½ tsp ground flax seed

2 tbsp walnuts or almonds, chopped

2 tbsp raisins

*Directions:*

Rinse quinoa and drain. Place water and quinoa into a small saucepan and bring to a boil. Add cinnamon and vanilla.

Reduce heat to low and simmer for about 15 minutes stirring often. When ready, place a portion of the quinoa into a bowl, drizzle with brown sugar and top with flax seeds, raisins and crushed walnuts.

# Citrus Quinoa Breakfast

*Serves: 2*
*Ingredients:*

½ cup quinoa

1 cup water

1 orange, peeled, cut into bite-sized pieces

2 tbsp blanched almonds, chopped

2 tbsp cranberries

1 tsp lemon zest

½ tsp vanilla

*Directions:*

Rinse quinoa and drain. Place water and quinoa into a small saucepan and bring to a boil. Add vanilla and lemon zest.

Reduce heat to low and simmer for about 15 minutes stirring often.

When ready, place a portion of the quinoa into a bowl and top with orange segments, cranberries and almonds.

# Avocado and Olive Paste on Toasted Rye Bread

*Serves: 4*
*Ingredients:*

1 avocado, peeled and finely chopped

2 tbsp black olive paste

1 tbsp lemon juice

*Directions:*

Mash avocados with a fork or potato masher until almost smooth. Add the black olive paste and lemon juice. Season with salt and pepper to taste. Stir to combine.

Toast 4 slices of rye bread until golden. Spoon 1/4 of the avocado mixture onto each slice of bread.

# Avocado, Lettuce and Tomato Sandwiches

*Serves: 2*
*Ingredients:*

4 slices wholewheat bread

1 tbsp vegan basil pesto

2 large leaves lettuce

1/2 tomato, thinly sliced

1/2 avocado, peeled and sliced

6 slices cucumber

*Directions:*

Spread pesto on the four slices of bread.

Layer two slices with one lettuce leaf, two slices tomato, two slices avocado and three slices cucumber.

Top with remaining bread slices. Cut sandwiches in half and serve.

# Avocado and Chickpea Sandwiches

*Serves: 4*
*Ingredients:*

4 slices rye bread

1/2 can chickpeas, drained

1 avocado

2-3 green onions, finely chopped

1/2 tomato, thinly sliced

1/3 tsp cumin

salt, to taste

*Directions:*

Mash the avocado and chickpeas with a fork or potato masher until smooth. Add in green onions, cumin and salt and combine well.

Spread this mixture on the four slices of bread. Top each slice with tomato and serve.

# Winter Greens Smoothie

*Serves: 2*
*Ingredients:*

2 broccoli florets, frozen

1½ cup coconut water

½ banana

½ cup pineapple

1 cup fresh spinach

2 kale leaves

*Directions:*

Combine ingredients in blender and blend until smooth. Enjoy!

# Delicious Kale Smoothie

*Serves: 2*
*Ingredients:*

2-3 ice cubes

1½ cup apple juice

3-4 kale leaves

1 apple, cut

1 cup strawberries

½ tsp cloves

*Directions:*

Combine ingredients in blender and purée until smooth.

# Cherry Smoothie

*Serves: 2*
*Ingredients:*

2-3 ice cubes

1½ cup almond or coconut milk

1½ cup pitted and frozen cherries

½ avocado

1 tsp cinnamon

1 tsp chia seeds

*Directions:*

Combine all ingredients into a blender and process until smooth. Enjoy!

# Banana and Coconut Smoothie

*Serves: 2*
*Ingredients:*

1 frozen banana, chopped

1½ cup coconut water

2-3 small broccoli florets

1 tbsp coconut butter

*Directions:*

Add all ingredients into a blender and blend until the smoothie turns into an even and smooth consistency. Enjoy!

# Vegan Walnut Pie

*Serves: 15*
*Ingredients:*

14 oz filo pastry

1 cup ground walnuts

2/3 cup melted plant-based butter

**For the syrup:**

2 cups sugar

2 cups water

1 tbsp vanilla powder

2 tbsp lemon zest

*Directions:*

Grease a baking tray and place 2-3 sheets of pastry. Crush the walnuts and spread some evenly on the pastry. Place two more sheets of the filo pastry on top.

Repeat until all the pastry sheets and walnuts have been used up. Always finish with some sheets of pastry on top.

Cut the pie in the tray into small squares. Melt the butter and pour it over the pie. Bake in a preheated oven at 350 F until light brown. When ready set aside to cool.

the syrup: Combine water and sugar in a saucepan. Add vanilla and lemon zest and bring to the boil, then lower the heat and simmer for about 5 minutes until the syrup is nearly thick. Pour hot syrup over the cold baked pie, leave to stand for at least 1-2 days until completely dry.

# Baked Apples

*Serves: 4*
*Ingredients:*

8 medium sized apples

1/3 cup walnuts, crushed

3/4 cup sugar

3 tbsp raisins, soaked

vanilla, cinnamon according to taste

*Directions:*

Peel and carefully hollow the apples. Prepare the stuffing by mixing 3/4 cup of sugar, crushed walnuts, raisins and cinnamon.

Stuff the apples and place in an oiled dish, pour over 1-2 tbsp of water and bake in a moderate oven. Serve warm.

# Blueberry Yogurt Dessert

*Serves 6*
*Ingredients:*

1/2 cup blueberry jam

1 cup fresh blueberries

1 cup heavy cream

2 tbsp powdered sugar

2 cups yogurt

*Directions:*

Strain the yogurt in a piece of cheesecloth or a clean white dishtowel. You can suspend it over a bowl or the sink.

In a large bowl, beat the cream and powdered sugar until soft peaks form. Add strained yogurt and beat until medium peaks form and the mixture is creamy and thick.

Gently fold half the fresh blueberries and the blueberry jam into cream mixture until just barely combined, with streaks remaining. Divide dessert among 6 glass bowls, top with fresh blueberries and serve.

# Fresh Strawberries in Mascarpone and Rose Water

*Serves 4*
*Ingredients:*

6 oz strawberries, washed

1 cup mascarpone cheese

1/2 teaspoon rose water

1/2 teaspoon vanilla extract

1/4 cup white sugar

*Directions:*

In a bowl, combine together the mascarpone cheese, sugar, rose water and vanilla.

Divide the strawberries into 4 dessert bowls. Add two dollops of mascarpone mixture on top and serve.

# Apple Cake

*Serves: 12*
*Ingredients:*

4-5 medium apples, sliced, cooked and mashed

1 cup walnuts, chopped

1/2 cup apple cider

1/2 cup sunflower oil

3 1/2 cups flour

1 1/2 cups sugar

1 tbsp baking powder

1/2 tsp baking soda, a pinch of salt

1 tsp cinnamon

1 /2 tsp fresh ground cardamom

1/2 tsp ground cloves

*Directions:*

Combine flour, baking powder, baking soda and salt.

In another bowl, mix sugar, vegetable oil and apple cider, until well blended. Add in spices and stir again. In a smaller bowl, mash cooked apples. Add apples to liquid ingredients and mix well.

Add dry ingredients to wet ingredients, stirring. Add walnuts and combine everything well.

Spread batter evenly in a lined 9×13" baking pan. Bake in a preheated to 350 F oven for 40 minutes. When completely cooled, dust with powdered sugar and cut.

# Pumpkin Baked with Dry Fruit

*Serves: 5-6*
*Ingredients:*

1.5 lb pumpkin, cut into medium pieces

1 cup dry fruit (apricots, plums, apples, raisins)

1/2 cup brown sugar

*Directions:*

Soak the dry fruit in some water, drain and discard the water. Cut the pumpkin in medium cubes.

At the bottom of a pot arrange a layer of pumpkin pieces, then a layer of dry fruit and then again some pumpkin. Add a little water.

Cover the pot and bring to boil. Simmer until there is no more water left. When almost ready add the sugar. Serve warm or cold.

# Pumpkin Pastry

*Serves: 8*
*Ingredients:*

14 oz filo pastry

14 oz pumpkin

1 cup walnuts, coarsely chopped

1/2 cup sugar

6 tbsp sunflower oil

1 tbsp cinnamon

1 tsp vanilla

1/3 cup powdered sugar

*Directions:*

Grate the pumpkin and steam it until tender. Cool and add the walnuts, sugar, cinnamon and vanilla. Place a few sheets of pastry in the baking dish, sprinkle with oil and spread the filling on top.

Repeat this a few times finishing with a sheet of pastry. Bake for 20 minutes at medium heat. Let the Pumpkin Pie cool down and dust with the powdered sugar.

# Apple Pastry

*Serves: 8*
*Ingredients:*

14 filo pastry

5-6 apples, peeled and cut

1 1/2 cup walnuts, coarsely chopped

2/3 cup sugar

6 tbsp oil

1 tbsp cinnamon

1/2 tsp vanilla extract

1/3 cup powdered sugar

*Directions:*

Cut the apples in small pieces and mix with the walnuts, sugar, cinnamon and vanilla. Place two sheets of pastry in the baking dish, sprinkle with oil and spread the filling on top.

Repeat this a few times finishing with a sheet of pastry. Bake for 20 minutes at medium heat. Let the Apple Pastry cool down and dust with the powdered sugar.

# Pumpkin Cake

*Serves: 12*
*Ingredients:*

2 cups grated pumpkin

1 1/2 cup sugar

1 tsp cinnamon

1/2 cup sunflower oil

1 cup warm water

1 cup ground walnuts

3 cups plain flour

1 tbsp baking powder

1/3 cup powdered sugar

*Directions:*

Combine sugar and grated pumpkin with cinnamon and leave for 15 minutes to absorb the aroma. Add oil and mix well with a fork. Add warm water and the crushed walnuts stirring well. Mix well the baking powder with the flour and gently add to the dough.

Preheat oven to 350 F. Pour the dough in an oiled and floured 9×13" baking pan. Bake for about 35 minutes. When ready and cold turn over a plate and sprinkle with powdered sugar.

# Granny's Vegan Cake

*Serves: 12*
*Ingredients:*

1/2 cup sugar

1 cup fruit jam

1 cup cool water

1/2 cup vegetable oil

1 cup crushed walnuts

1 tsp baking soda

2 1/2 cups flour

1 tsp vanilla powder

½ tsp cinnamon

*Directions:*

Combine the baking soda with the jam and leave for 10 min. Add sugar, water, oil, walnuts and flour in that order.

Mix well and pour in a round 10 x 2-inches cake pan.

Bake in a preheated to 350 F oven. When ready turn over a plate and sprinkle with powdered sugar.

**About the Author**

Vesela Tabakova lives in Bulgaria with her family of five, a crazy Jack Russell Terrier and three adopted dogs.

Reading is her passion and coffee is her drug of choice. She loves cooking and preparing natural, homemade beauty products for family and friends.

Her inspiration comes from many tried and tested recipes which circulate within her extended family, but she also experiments all the time in order to create new and varied recipes, better suited to modern tastes.

Printed in Great Britain
by Amazon